CHARLES E. CURRAN

THE CHURCH AND MORALITY

An Ecumenical and Catholic Approach

FORTRESS PRESS Minneapolis

To
family and friends
especially those who have gathered
in summer on the dunes

Jan and Ernest
Christa, Matt, Benita, Beth
Colleen and David
Bill

THE CHURCH AND MORALITY
An Ecumenical and Catholic Approach

Cover design: Pollock Design Group
Interior design: The Book Company/Wendy Calmenson

Library of Congress Cataloging-in-Publication Data

Curran, Charles E.
The Church and morality : an ecumenical and Catholic approach / Charles E. Curran.
p. cm.
"Based on the 1991–1992 Hein/Fry Lecture Series sponsored by the Evangelical Lutheran Church in America."
Includes bibliographical references.
ISBN 0-8006-2756-3 (alk. paper)
1. Christian ethics—Catholic authors. 2. Church—Catholicity. 3. Catholic Church—Relations. 4. Catholic Church—Doctrines. I. Title.
BJ1249.C813 1993
241'.042—dc20 92-47448
CIP

The paper used in this publication meets the minimum requirements of American National Standard for Information Sciences—Permanence of Paper for Printed Library Materials, ANSI Z329.48-1984. ∞™

Manufactured in the U.S.A. AF 1–2756

97 96 95 94 93 1 2 3 4 5 6 7 8 9 10

CONTENTS

PREFACE

THIS BOOK IS BASED ON THE 1991–92 HEIN/FRY LECTURE Series sponsored by the Evangelical Lutheran Church in America (ELCA). The governing committee of this endowed lectureship invited Larry L. Rasmussen of Union Theological Seminary in New York and me to present a separate series of lectures hosted by the eight seminaries of the ELCA. I am grateful to the committee for its kind invitation to inaugurate this lecture series and most appreciative of the gracious hospitality and discussion of my lectures provided by four Lutheran seminaries, in Philadelphia, St. Paul, Dubuque, and Columbus.

The general area of the topic—the church and morality—has been a continuing concern for me, and I was most grateful to have the opportunity to address the question. Most mainstream churches in the United States today struggle with the issue of how the church learns and teaches its approach to morality, and their national meetings in the last few years have reflected this. Division over moral issues has affected the unity of many of these churches. Acrimonious debates take place within the churches and leave people confused and angry.

The churches' moral authority also seems to be eroding in

our society. Many people no longer look to the churches for moral guidance. Some claim that the churches must be in dialogue with the present culture, while others insist that the church needs to oppose any cultural adaptation by repeating its traditional moral teachings with even greater zeal and certainty.

The topic of the church and morality involves not only the internal moral life of the church but also the role of the church in the moral life of society and the nation. All recognize the manifold moral problems facing our country and our world today. The Christian gospel calls for Christians as the community of the disciples of Jesus to work for a more free, just, and peaceful world. But great divisions exist within and among the churches on many of these issues. Here too the question acutely arises about unity and diversity within the individual church and among the churches. Where should there be unity within the church, and where should there be diversity?

The topic of the role of the churches in American public life becomes even more complex in the light of the important distinction between morality and legality and especially in the light of the First Amendment separation of church and state. What is a proper involvement of churches in American public life? The topic of the church and morality addresses issues of primary concern for the churches themselves and also for the broader society.

The ecumenical aspect of the topic is most intriguing. The Evangelical Lutheran Church in America invited me as a Roman Catholic moral theologian to address this topic. The basic tensions surrounding the topic of the church and morality are common to many different church bodies today. An ecumenical approach recognizes the common elements in the issue shared by a good number of churches and denominations.

Yes, many different churches share the same basic tensions and problems in dealing with their own internal moral life and with their relationship to the moral issues facing the broader American and human society. The question arises whether there exists something in common that many different churches share, and which can shed some light on how the churches should deal with these tensions. In this book I propose that such a common understanding does exist. The subtitle of the volume, *An Ecumenical and Catholic Approach,* indicates that in my judgment most mainstream Christian churches in the United States share a catholic approach to their moral role and function. As will be made clear in the text itself, this catholicity is spelled with a small *c.* On the basis of this common understanding of catholicity, the volume proposes how the churches should learn, teach, and propose their own moral approaches and how they should relate to the moral issues facing the broader society.

Such an ecumenical perspective has the advantage of addressing many different churches and facilitating dialogue among the churches on how to understand and structure their approach to morality. At the same time such an approach also eliminates very thorny questions of the polities, structures, and processes by which individual churches arrive at their moral teachings. The locus of authority differs very much from church to church, even among those churches that share the same basic catholic approach. The ecumenical perspective of these lectures and of this volume means that the particular ecclesiological differences of the individual churches do not have to be treated. No small volume could ever do justice to these diverse ecclesiologies.

In keeping with the intention of the lecture series, I hope that this volume contributes something to the individual churches and to the ecumenical dialogue in general about how the mainstream churches deal with moral realities in the life of their community and the broader human society.

My position as Elizabeth Scurlock University Professor of Human Values at Southern Methodist University has provided me the time and the resources to research and write this volume. I am most grateful to all who have facilitated and aided my work. Jack and Laura Lee Blanton funded this chair in honor of Mrs. Blanton's mother as a further sign of their strong commitment to higher education in general and of their continuing and generous support of Southern Methodist University in particular. My colleagues in the Perkins School of Theology and in the Department of Religious Studies of Dedman College have discussed and criticized parts of this book. The librarians of the Bridwell Library have graciously assisted me in many ways. Above all, on a day-to-day basis, my associate and administrative assistant Jane Cross has gracefully and competently supported my scholarly endeavors in general and has prepared this manuscript for publication. Julia Fleming has graciously and competently prepared the index.

CHAPTER 1

The Criterion of Catholicity and the Church Catholic

ALL MUST AGREE THAT THE CHURCH CONSTITUTES A COMMUNITY of moral conviction. The church is the community of the disciples of the risen Jesus who gather through the Spirit to celebrate in word and sacrament and to live out the life of discipleship. The cornerstone of the Christian church involves a faith commitment to Jesus and to the community. Moral convictions flow from this. The follower of Jesus is committed in general to discipleship and to living out the reality of the Christian life.

Many more particular moral convictions characterize the life of the members of the Christian community. Love has often been described as a distinctive and fundamental Christian moral attitude. Christian love involves a universality that includes all and constantly strives to go beyond the limits of the present. Love of enemies, mercy, forgiveness, and compassion all flow from Christian love. The follower of Jesus is committed to the way of Jesus and all entailed in that discipleship. Hope in the power and promise of God gives dynamism to the Christian life. Like Jesus, the Christian is committed to a love and concern for the needy, the poor, the marginalized, and the outcast. Justice calls for the follower of Jesus to give others their due. Those who believe that a gracious God created the world for the use of all God's people share the conviction that the goods of creation exist to serve the needs of all. Social and political systems must strive for a justice that protects and promotes all people in society and the ecosystem itself. We are stewards of the goods of creation and must not abuse them but use them for their God-given purpose to support the needs of all. Yes, all Christians can and should agree that the church constitutes a community of moral conviction.

But the church involves more than a community of moral conviction. In fact the church often shows itself to be the opposite—a community of moral doubt. Consider the experience of so many Christian churches today. Our moral life is often characterized by doubts and even divisions. We disagree about the proper role of the military in our society, the best ways to provide for the poor, the proper distribution of the goods and burdens of our human existence. Disagreements exist also about personal moral teachings. The abortion issue has occasioned bitter disputes in our churches. Issues connected with sexuality have divided our churches on all levels—local, national, and universal. All the mainstream churches in the United States have experienced some divisions on sexual issues such as homosexuality.

Despite the often shrill debates and discussions, a *modus vivendi* frequently occurs depending on the polity and discipline of the particular churches. Even in more structural churches, such as the Roman Catholic, individuals will continue to do in their own private lives what they believe is right as they continue to share in the life of the church. Doubt and discussion become more acrimonious when the community itself must take a united stand, as, for example, in the qualities required for a minister. Many church members experience the reality of doubt and division within the church more frequently and more intensely than they experience the reality of the church as a community of moral conviction.

The problem is not confined only to the contemporary church. A sensitive reading of Christian Scripture reveals that the early Christian communities experienced many different controversies that often involved moral issues or actions. One example is the dispute over the observance of the Jewish law. Could the followers of Jesus eat meat that had been sacrificed to idols? Tensions arose in the early communities over the proper care of widows. Questions of marriage and remarriage also raised some doubts and differences. The imminent coming of the fullness of God's reign occasioned contradictory approaches. Some reasoned that in such a context there was no need to work and provide for the future. Eating and drinking to excess and not sharing with others characterized the behavior of some Christians even at the agape meal. True, the Christian Scriptures generally talk about the problems after they were solved, but a critical reading cannot forget the tensions and divisions that existed before the acceptable solutions were proposed and agreed upon by the community. From the earliest times the community of the disciples of Jesus has experienced doubts, tensions, and controversies over its behavior and actions.

The church truly constitutes a community of moral conviction; but the disciples of Jesus also know doubts, tensions, and differences about what is morally required and acceptable behavior. The problem immediately arises: How does the church community distinguish its convictions from its doubts?

The church is also called to be a community of moral praxis. The Christian is called to the following of Jesus, and the church is the community of discipleship. By this very commitment Christians dedicate themselves to bearing witness to Jesus. By their fruits you will know them. Not everyone who says "Lord, Lord" will enter into the reign of God. In John's Gospel the farewell address of Jesus to the disciples reminds them to love one another as Jesus has loved them. The so-called last judgment scene in Matthew 25 insists that our ultimate relationship to God is known, manifested, and judged by our actions toward our neighbor in need. The distinctive Christian love commandment is found in all three Synoptic Gospels—love God with one's whole heart, mind, body, and soul, and love your neighbor as yourself.

Some aspects of contemporary theology firmly insist on the importance of action and praxis. In the past the Christian tradition has put primary emphasis on orthodoxy, or proper belief, but the Christian community also needs orthopraxis or proper actions. In my judgment both orthopraxis and orthodoxy are required of the members of the church community.

Praxis consists in more than just action.[1] Praxis refers to a way of human knowing in which our actions contribute to our knowledge. Knowledge is not just rationalistic, conceptual, and the result of observation by a neutral, noninvolved party. In this perspective not only are actions important but they also contribute to the human knowing process.

Even those who reject the more technical notion of praxis still must recognize that the Christian community must be a community of action. Hence the problem arises again: What actions are to be done, and what actions are to be avoided?

The fact that the church is a community of doubt as well as a community of conviction, and the recognition that the

[1]Clodovis Boff, *Theology and Praxis: Epistemological Foundations* (Maryknoll, N.Y.: Orbis Books, 1987); see also Matthew L. Lamb, *Solidarity with Victims: Toward a Theology of Social Transformation* (New York: Crossroad, 1982).

church must decide what actions to do and what actions to avoid, point to the prior need for the church to discern and distinguish its convictions from its doubts, its proper actions from those that contradict its mission. At a more basic level the church constitutes a community of moral discourse attempting to discern and live out what is in keeping with its self-understanding and mission.

Moral discernment is required, and the church as a community arrives at this discernment through moral discourse. Discourse needs to be understood as broadly encompassing more than just intellectual discussion. The moral discourse of the Christian community involves all the members of the community attempting to discern in every way possible what is to be done.

This volume thus recognizes many significant aspects about the moral reality of the church community, but the most fundamental and basic reality refers to the church as a community of moral discourse.[2] Subsequent considerations will concentrate on the church as a community of moral discourse and propose how that community should go about its moral discernment and its moral life.

The Common Criterion of Catholicity

THE TOPIC OF THE CHURCH AS A MORAL COMMUNITY EMBRACES three significant theological areas: ecclesiology; the moral teaching, convictions, and life of the church with regard to its

[2]For an earlier development of the church as a community of moral discourse, see James M. Gustafson, *The Church as Moral Decision Maker* (Philadelphia: Pilgrim Press, 1970). For an approach similar to the one taken in these pages, see Larry L. Rasmussen, "Going Public: The Church's Roles," in *God, Goods, and the Common Good,* ed. Charles P. Lutz (Minneapolis: Augsburg, 1987), 28–43.

own internal life and members; and the moral teaching, convictions, and actions with regard to the wider pluralistic society in which we all live. Our comprehensive development of the topic will include these three different areas.

From a theological perspective these three different areas are not totally disparate. The position taken in one's ecclesiology is logically connected with the positions proposed with regard to the moral teachings and internal life of the church and its moral teaching and actions with regard to the broader society. Many of the same theological presuppositions involved in ecclesiology often play a role in understanding the moral life of the community of faith and its relationship to the moral life of society as a whole.

Ernst Troeltsch's classical discussion of the sect shows how these three areas are intimately connected.[3] The sectarian model, especially in its Anabaptist origins, places a strong emphasis on discipleship. The Christian is called to a radical following of Christ Jesus. The individual Christian lives out the response to the gospel in a community of disciples who embrace this radical ethic. In contradistinction to the church type, the sect does not try to embrace all humankind. Believers' baptism and not infant baptism marks the entrance rite of the individual into this community of discipleship. Its intense moral approach rests on a commitment to a radical following of the will of God as exemplified in the ethical teaching of Jesus found especially in the Sermon on the Mount. The commitment to this morality within a small dedicated community separates the sectarian from others, and especially from the world. Life in the world is not compatible with the life of discipleship. Life in the world involves the need to take

[3]Ernst Troeltsch, *The Social Teaching of the Christian Churches,* vol. 2 (New York: Harper Torchbooks, 1960), 691–729.

oaths and to use force and violence. The state itself is above all characterized by this use of force. The world, and especially the state, are not touched by God's redeeming love but are primarily the area of sin and the demonic. Hence sectarians have to separate themselves from the world and live apart by themselves in their small communities. The internal structure of the sect, its moral teaching for its own members, and its relationship to the world form an integral and consistent whole.

In discussing the church as a moral community, I intend to describe our understanding of what is common to many different churches and denominations. I come out of the Roman Catholic tradition and am addressing in the first place the Evangelical Lutheran Church in America about the church as a community of moral discourse. I want to address many different churches and denominations by stressing what is common to them without denying that each has distinctive and unique features.

What is envisioned here is similar to what Martin Marty did in his book on the public church.[4] Professor Marty describes the public church as a family of apostolic churches with Jesus Christ as the center and with a concern for the public order that embraces all in our American pluralistic society. This public church is a communion of communions, each of which lives its life partly in response to its separate tradition and partly in response to the call for a common Christian witness and vocation in the wider society. The public church in the United States today, according to Marty, comprises three components—the Catholic, mainline Protestants, and Evangelical Protestants. Each of these three com-

[4]Martin E. Marty, *The Public Church: Mainline—Evangelical—Catholic* (New York: Crossroad, 1981).

ponent groups within itself has its differences and tensions, but all today come under the rubric of the public church. Evangelical Protestants have been the last component to join this public church with their concern for what is happening in our society and world. Professor Marty describes the way in which the public church should act and respond to the concerns, issues, and problems in society.

I fundamentally agree with Marty's thesis. Under this somewhat broad umbrella he has astutely pointed out the attitudes and approaches that should characterize the public church in its ongoing dialogue with society. In this book I am attempting to do something more inclusive than what Professor Marty did—a discussion not only of the public church as the relationship of the church to the broader pluralistic society but also some understanding of the church itself and of the way in which the church goes about shaping its own internal moral life and convictions. The public church portrays an apt and accurate understanding of the reality Marty is describing. Is there an apt and accurate description that adequately and consistently explains the approach that many churches and denominations take to the understanding of (1) the church itself from a moral perspective, (2) the internal moral thought, life, and actions of the church and its members, (3) the approach of the church and its members to the moral thinking and life of the broader pluralistic society?

As I mentioned before, I believe a relationship exists among these three different areas, so that one's understanding of the church is logically consistent with one's approach to the community's internal moral life and to the community's relationship to the moral life of the broader society. Is there a concept similar to Martin Marty's public church that provides a coherent understanding of the approach the churches take to these three different realities that still acknowledges the churches' significant differences?

I suggest the concept that brings all these three realities together in a coherent and systematic way and gives direction and shape to our understanding of the issues involved is catholicity—and I hasten to add with a small *c*. One immediate problem with such a concept comes from the fact that Catholic with capital *C* has become the way that Roman Catholicism often designates itself as distinct from the other Christian churches. This designation arose from an institutional and apologetic need of Roman Catholicism from the sixteenth through the nineteenth century to distinguish itself from all other churches as the one, true church of Jesus Christ. The four marks of the church—one, holy, catholic, and apostolic—are found only in the Roman Catholic Church. However, in the nineteenth and especially in the twentieth century, Catholic theologians began to recover a broader sense of catholicity. Such an understanding of the concept of catholicity is very evident in the teachings of the Second Vatican Council.[5] Contemporary Roman Catholicism thus recognizes two different understandings of catholicity and does not claim to have a monopoly on it.

Mainstream Christian churches have accepted the early creeds of the church with their insistence on catholicity. The Nicene-Constantinopolitan Creed professes belief in the church—one, holy, catholic, and apostolic.[6] Contemporary ecumenical discussion insists on catholicity. The Fourth Assembly of the World Council of Churches meeting in Upsala

[5]Avery Dulles, *The Catholicity of the Church* (Oxford: Clarendon Press, 1985); see also Dulles, "Catholicism," in *The New Dictionary of Theology,* ed. Joseph A. Komonchak et al. (Wilmington, Del.: Michael Glazier, 1987), 167–72.
[6]*Enchiridion Symbolorum Definitionum et Declarationum de Rebus Fidei et Morum,* 32d ed., ed. H. Denzinger et al. (Barcelona: Herder, 1963), n. 150, pp. 66, 67.

maintained that the church is and should be catholic in all her elements and in all aspects of her life.[7] Thus the concept of catholicity is common to many Christian churches.

What does catholicity mean and involve? At the present time there seems to be no exact definition or description upon which all readily agree. History also reminds us of the analogical use of the term *catholic*—even with a small *c*. Jaroslav Pelikan has proposed that catholicity emerged in the early centuries and is characterized by five elements that were seminally present from the beginning—missionary expansion, church organization with an ordered episcopal ministry, church life involving a sacramental system, theology with its standards of orthodoxy (e.g., creeds and canonical Scriptures), and a *modus vivendi* with the broader society and the secular state.[8]

Avery Dulles has written a very helpful monograph on catholicity in which he too distinguishes between catholicity with a small *c* and Catholicity with a capital *C*. Dulles distinguishes and develops four salient features of catholicity with a small *c* under the analogies of height, depth, breadth, and length.[9]

For the purposes of the present discussion we need an understanding of catholicity that will generally be accepted by the large number of the churches and denominations that seem to share the same general approach with regard to the

---

[7] *The Upsala Report,* ed. Norman Goodall (Geneva: World Council of Churches, 1968), 11–18. See also *Catholicity and Apostolicity,* a special issue of *One in Christ* 6/3 (1970), and Patrick W. Fuerth, *The Concept of Catholicity in the Documents of the World Council of Churches (1948–1968)* (Rome: Anselmiana, 1973).

[8] Jaroslav Pelikan, *The Riddle of Roman Catholicism* (Nashville: Abingdon Press, 1959), 21–33.

[9] Dulles, *Catholicity of the Church,* 30–105.

moral life of the Christian community and its relationship to society. I propose three characteristics of such a catholicity. One, the church is universal in the sense of open to all humanity. Two, the faith of the church strives to penetrate all dimensions of existence. Three, catholicity involves a union of many different aspects, some of which might even seem to be opposed to one another, and does not call for a rigid uniformity. A brief elaboration of these three characteristics will offer a clearer idea of why I think these three characteristics belong to a basic concept of catholicity.

The first two characteristics are really based on the etymology of the word *catholic*. It has always had this dimension of universality about it and likewise the aspect of penetrating all dimensions of existence. Martin Marty has briefly mentioned these as the two fundamental characteristics of catholicity.[10] I believe that these two characteristics are generally acceptable to most people who would maintain the catholicity of the church to which they give allegiance.

The third characteristic at the very minimum tries to avoid a danger that in my judgment has at times been associated with Roman Catholicism.[11] The danger in an attempt to be universal and to embrace all dimensions of existence involves a too easy reach for a uniformity that fails to be truly catholic in respecting the many differences that exist within a general unity. Avery Dulles develops this aspect of catholicity in some detail. True catholicity does not exclude differences but demands them. Catholicity involves a union of opposites that might even seem to be incompatible. Trinitarian and christological warrants compel this characteristic of catholicity to recognize and support differences and to avoid flatten-

[10]Marty, *The Public Church,* 31.
[11]See Charles Curran, *Living Tradition of Catholic Moral Theology* (Notre Dame, Ind.: University of Notre Dame Press, 1992).

ing out such differences in a facile demand of uniformity. The Trinity itself involves both unity and diversity. The fundamental mystery is how the three remain distinct but are still one. Likewise the mystery of the incarnation brings together the divine and the human without in any way trying to absorb or flatten out the great differences between them.[12]

These three characteristics of catholicity will help us understand the meaning of catholicity as applied to the church, its development of morality for itself, and its relationship to the moral thinking and life of the pluralistic society in which we live.

This book attempts to speak across church and denominational lines and thus constitutes an exercise in ecumenical theology. I believe that many mainstream churches share an understanding of the church, its internal moral life, and its relationship to society based on the concept of catholicity. Many churches share the same general approach here and can and should be in dialogue with one another in their attempt to live out this reality of the church catholic. However, by definition the considerations that are common to many mainstream churches will leave out significant areas of disagreement. Thus, for example, I will not deal here with the thorny issue of the particular locus of authority within the community of the church. Different churches have different positions and understandings of about who or what constitutes the church's moral authority. Whether the authority in moral matters resides in a particular assembly or group of officeholders lies beyond the scope of this book. By striving to be ecumenical and embracing in a general way the mainstream Christian churches, these considerations will bracket and avoid the particularities that divide these churches.

---

[12]Dulles, *Catholicity of the Church,* 31–34.

Catholicity and Ecclesiology

For our purposes one need not develop a full-blown ecclesiology but only sketch those aspects that pertain to an understanding of the church as a moral community both for its own members and internal life and for its external life in society. Even here only those aspects held in common by many churches will be mentioned.

The catholicity of the church involves three characteristics: an inclusive community open to all and appealing to all; different levels of church, including both the local and the universal; and a recognition that the members of the church community also belong to many other communities and institutions. In a certain sense these three characteristics illustrate the inclusive tendencies of a catholicity that tries not to exclude but to bring many aspects together in a broader unity. Such a catholic approach tends to insist on both-and and rejects an either-or approach.

The church is a universal community open to all and appealing to all. The universalism of the community of the disciples of Jesus is grounded in the Scriptures themselves. There is no need to recall all the biblical passages here. Galatians 3:28 has often been quoted as illustrating such universality—there is neither Jew nor Greek, slave nor free, male nor female in Christ Jesus. The Gospel of Matthew closes with the mission of the apostles to make disciples of all nations.

The membership of the church is not perfect or without sin or spot. The church is not the small group of the perfect but is open to all. Thus infant baptism characterizes the churches that are catholic in distinction from the believers' baptism of the sects. However, even some churches who practice adult baptism are today truly catholic in their self-understanding and structure. All churches that are catholic in one way or another recognize that the members of their communities are not perfect and are to some extent sinners. Such an inclusive and catholic community is distinguished from the sect with its emphasis on the small community of the perfect who follow a radical gospel ethic.

The catholic church community not only includes saints and sinners but also should embrace all in terms of race, class, and gender. Here too the historical reality reminds us of how often the church has fallen short of this vision. Contemporary liberation theologians in Latin America and other parts of the world have pointed out how readily the poor have been forgotten and oppressed.[13] Likewise feminist theologians have reminded us of the patriarchy that has so often characterized the life of the church even in our day.[14] However, those great problems existing within the church stand in opposition to the professed belief in catholicity as including all and, above all, not trying to reduce all to a false uniformity.

Historically the church has had a spatial aspect to its catholicity, as illustrated in the missionary movements. The catholic church thus is a universal and worldwide community that is open to all persons, all places, and all cultures. The church catholic cannot be restricted to any one culture. History, and especially recent history, indicates the perennial temptation of identifying the church with a particular culture.[15] The church must become inculturated in its own par-

---

[13] *Liberation Theology: A Documentary History,* ed. Alfred Hennelly (Maryknoll, N.Y.: Orbis Press, 1990).

[14] *Struggles for Solidarity: Liberation Theologyies in Tension,* ed. Lorine M. Getz and Ruy O. Costa (Minneapolis: Fortress Press, 1991).

[15] Aylward Shorter, *Toward a Theology of Inculturation* (Maryknoll, N.Y.: Orbis Books, 1988).

ticular circumstances without, however, ceasing to be the community of the disciples of Jesus.

A second consequence of a catholicity that is both universal and all-embracing concerns the various embodiments of church. The church is universal, but it is also local. The church is primarily the local community that gathers together to celebrate in word and sacrament and to live the life-giving love of God in Jesus and the Spirit. Much disagreement exists about the nature of the church universal, but all recognize that the church is more than the local church. Likewise the exact relationship between the local and universal church is disputed.

Both theology and history testify to the problems arising from an overemphasis on the local church to the exclusion of the universal dimension. The great temptation of all human beings consists in using God and religion for one's own purposes. The great idolatry involves making God into our image and likeness. Look at the many different ways in which Jesus has been understood and interpreted throughout history—as a capitalist, a Marxist, a revolutionary, a terrorist, a patriot, an obedient servant, and others. Contemporary feminist theology reminds us of the temptation and reality of patriarchy whereby God is identified as a male. The history of Christianity in the United States indicates the divisions that arose in this country over the Civil War, some of which have never been healed and overcome.[16] A universal church with a universal perspective serves as a criticism of the pretensions of any individual, group, race, or gender to absolutize its own perspective. Too often in the United States we

---

[16]C. C. Goen, *Broken Churches, Broken Nation: Denominational Schisms and the Coming of the American Civil War* (Mercer, Ga.: Mercer University Press, 1985).

have insisted that God is on our side in all that we do, and especially in our wars. We too must constantly recognize the danger of these narrow perspectives that can so easily distort the Christian message. The catholicity of the church and the recognition that we belong to a universal community serves as a strong self-criticism and impels us to question a too quick identification of our cause with God.

On the other hand, a one-sided emphasis on universality results in that static uniformity which fails to recognize the necessary diversity that must always be a part of catholicity. The recent history of Christianity has made us more aware of the dangers of identifying the church universal with Western Christianity and failing to recognize that Christianity, if it is truly catholic, must become incarnate in all cultures. The concept of catholicity keeps the seeming opposition of particular and universal in a dynamic tension and reconciliation. Of course a tension will always exist between the church local and the church universal, but catholicity supplies a higher, transcendent unity embracing the seeming opposites and offers some general criteria for understanding the reconciliation of these two aspects.

The tension between the first two characteristics of catholicity with regard to ecclesiology is even more pronounced in the local church. How can the local church, which exists in a very particular time and place, be truly universal and embrace all? Obviously it cannot. However, the local church must be open to embrace all and recognize its relationship to the church universal. The catholicity of the local church will always involve a spirit and a vision rather than an actual reality, but such vision and spirit remain absolutely necessary. The local church can never become a club of like-minded people similar to so many other clubs that bring together people of the same background, same class, same race, same ethnic tradition. The call to embrace all remains a challenge and a stimulus to the local church and should constantly influence its life and practice. The local church recognizes its narrowness and strives to avoid being trapped in it. Such a local church will always know and experience the tensions of being both local and catholic.

The mainstream churches that are truly catholic recognize that the local church relates itself to a broader ecclesial reality often on the national and international levels. These relationships exist not only for the churches with a high ecclesiology, such as the Roman Catholic, Eastern Orthodox, Anglican, and Lutheran, but also for the churches on the lower level of the ecclesiological scale, such as the Baptists. The ecclesiologies and polities of the individual churches or denominations understand and structure the relationship of the local church to the broader church in many different ways, but all recognize and emphasize such a catholic dimension to their existence.

In the midst of the present ecclesial realities, catholicity also implies a relationship to what might be called the ecumenical church, which includes all Christian churches that claim to be communities of the disciples of Jesus. Individual churches and denominations on every level of their existence also need to relate to the ecumenical movement and to all the other Christian churches and denominations.

A third characteristic of the catholicity of the church recognizes that individuals belong to many different groups, associations, and communities in addition to the church. From the perspective of catholicity, one's faith commitment in belonging to the community of the disciples of Jesus does not absorb all one's other commitments, associations, and communities. Here again we recognize that catholicity does not exclude the many other aspects of life but tries to bring them together into a higher synthesis and reconciliation. The religious commitment in general and membership in the Christian community in particular form not merely one among many other commitments but rather constitute the ultimate and the broadest commitment, including all the other commitments and associations that are part of one's life. The Christian commitment is of a more ultimate nature, which should give direction to the whole of one's life; but the Christian commitment itself can also learn much from the many other commitments and communities involved in our human existence.

The tension of the catholicity that recognizes our membership in differing communities and a somewhat dialogical relationship among these various communities is illustrated in many ways—for example, by the relationship between the Christian churches and the American culture in which we live. We are Christians; we are Americans. Parenthetically, I appeal for an adjective that corresponds to the noun *United States.* American is not an accurate description of people who live only in the United States of America and might well illustrate some of the arrogance and hubris that on more than one occasion have characterized us who live in the United States. All must recognize the danger of our Christian commitment's too readily being influenced and affected by the commitment to our national community. As a religious people we have a tendency to manipulate religious belief and symbols for our own purposes. From the days of our manifest destiny down through the cold war to the present we have too often surrendered to the temptation to use our Christianity to support very debatable national goals and plans.[17] The danger here is perennial, and vigilance is always called for.

---

[17]See, for example, Martin E. Marty, *Righteous Empire: The Protestant Experience in America* (New York: Dial Press, 1970); David J. O'Brien, *The Renewal of American Catholicism* (New York: Paulist Press, 1973).

The Christian commitment, although ultimate and all-embracing, exists in dialogue with our other commitments and communities. Christianity has been enriched by some things found in the ethos and culture of the United States of America. Here Christian religions learned respect for and appreciation of the dignity, freedom, and rights of individuals. Of course the Christian community must always be conscious of its need to scrutinize, criticize, and correct the culture; but the church catholic at times can and should learn from the culture in which it exists. Once again catholicity attempts not to absorb and deny differences but to live with the tension of diversity in the light of a more transcendent whole. The catholic churches recognize that at times they have learned from the experience of their members in and through the other communities and associations with which they are involved.

CHAPTER 2

Catholicity and the Internal Moral Life of the Church

WE HAVE CONSIDERED THE GENERAL UNDERSTANDING OF CHURCH from a catholic perspective and can now focus on the internal moral life of the church. Before our discussion turns to how the church should understand, structure, and live its moral life, two preliminary questions need to be explored—the sources of morality and the different levels of morality. In both cases a catholic approach influences how one understands such issues, although different approaches will continue to exist within the general parameters common to all who accept a general catholic perspective.

The Sources of Morality

A CATHOLIC APPROACH THAT INVOLVES A THRUST TO PENETRATE all dimensions of existence will oppose more exclusive approaches to the sources of morality. A catholic approach will be open to both divine and human sources of knowledge. One can speak of these different sources as Scripture, tradition, human reason, and experience.[1] In general, catholic approaches employ

[1]Many catholic approaches would accept these four sources, but

all these sources in arriving at moral wisdom and knowledge, but disagreement exists about how these different sources relate to one another and contribute to the final moral judgment.

Since a catholic approach is opposed to exclusive approaches, our primary concern here is to show that an exclusive approach is not adequate. The exclusive approach that has often been associated with Christian morality concerns the Scripture alone. The catholic approach in general cannot accept that the Bible alone is the source of moral wisdom and knowledge for the Christian community.

Historically the axiom "the Scripture alone" has been associated with aspects of the Protestant Reformation and its differences from the Roman Catholic position. However, as Jaroslav Pelikan has pointed out, as a matter of fact the axiom "the Scripture alone" never really meant that in practice.[2] Especially in the area of morality, the Bible has never been the sufficient and sole basis for the understanding of morality within the mainstream Christian communities.[3]

On the contemporary scene the catholic approach to Scripture rejects any fundamentalism.[4] Not all nonfunda-

---

they constitute what has been called the Wesleyan Quadrilateral. However, this concept does not come from John Wesley but from the late Albert Outler, who coined it as a metaphor to understand Wesley's theological method. See Ted A. Campbell, "'The Wesleyan Quadrilateral': A Modern Methodist Myth," in *Theology in the United Methodist Church,* ed. Thomas G. Langford (Nashville: Kingswood Books, 1990), 154–61.

[2]Jaroslav Pelikan, *The Vindication of Tradition* (New Haven: Yale Univ. Press, 1984), ll; Pelikan, *The Christian Tradition*, 4: *Reformation of Church and Dogma (1300–1700)* (Chicago: University of Chicago Press, 1984), 127–82.

[3]Larry L. Rasmussen and Bruce C. Birch, *Bible and Ethics in the Christian Life,* rev. and expanded ed. (Minneapolis: Augsburg, 1989).

[4]Thomas F. O'Meara, *Fundamentalism: A Catholic Perspective* (New

mentalists agree on the meaning of Scripture, but all to some extent accept the historical-critical interpretation of the Scriptures. Fundamentalists tend to see Scripture as the inerrant word of God promulgated for all times and all places. Historical-critical method recognizes that the Scriptures are historically, linguistically, culturally, and socially conditioned, and these conditions are at least somewhat different from the conditions and times in which we live. If one accepts such an understanding of Scripture, then the insufficiency of the Bible alone as a source of moral wisdom and knowledge is evident.

The insufficiency of Scripture stands out especially in dealing with the morality of particular questions and issues. The differences between the biblical worlds and our contemporary context affect especially the concrete issues that greatly depend on their context, for example, the issue of how the civil government should be structured.

The most evident insufficiency of Scripture concerns the new moral issues that have arisen in our times. In medical ethics, for example, issues such as the withdrawal of feeding tubes or in vitro fertilization have arisen because of the tremendous scientific and technological developments that have occurred in our time.[5] The Scriptures obviously do not address these problems.

The greatly changed historical and cultural circumstances mean that specific moral directives found in the Scriptures might not be applicable or even helpful in today's world. Many contemporary Christian ethicists in the catholic tradi-

---

York: Paulist Press, 1990).

[5]See, for example, the rather complete anthology of *On Moral Medicine: Theological Perspectives in Medical Ethics,* ed. Stephen E. Lammers and Allen Verhey (Grand Rapids, Mich.: William B. Eerdmans, 1987).

tion even claim that some moral positions taken in the Scriptures should not be taken today. The attitude of the Scriptures to slavery has always caused problems for Christians.[6] At the very minimum the Christian Scriptures do not condemn the institution of slavery. The teaching on women and their roles in society, family, and the church as found in some Christian Scriptures have been strongly challenged by feminist theology. Feminist theory makes the point that patriarchal attitudes have colored and distorted the understanding of the role of women as found in the Christian Bible.[7] In other words, the good news also contains bad news. The moral positions found in the Scriptures can even be wrong as we look at them today. Not all Christian ethicists who embrace the broad catholic camp would be willing to recognize moral error in Scripture, but all must recognize the insufficiency of Scripture alone to deal with the moral issues facing our society today. However, as the next major section will point out, morality involves more than the determination of the morality of a particular act. In fact the role and contribution of Scripture will be much more significant in the more general moral questions of orientation, dispositions, and values.[8]

Many scholars from within the broad perspective of a catholic approach point out that the moral teaching found in the Bible itself is borrowed heavily from the morality of the times and the places of surrounding peoples. The Ten Commandments, which have retained a historic importance in both the Jewish and Christian traditions, show much similar-

---

[6]See, for example, John Francis Maxwell, *Slavery in the Catholic Church* (London: Barry Rose, 1975).
[7]Elisabeth Schüssler Fiorenza, *In Memory of Her: A Feminist Theological Reconstruction of Christian Origins* (New York: Crossroad, 1983).
[8]Rasmussen and Birch, *Bible and Ethics.*

ity with laws required for the good order of life in the civil society of the time. The wisdom sayings of the Hebrew Scriptures appear to be maxims of a more general character that can be embraced by all human beings. Even the prophetic writings have been understood as not primarily based on any content revealed by God in a special manner. The prophetic approach refined the traditionally accepted morality and stressed the centrality of good moral living, however its details were discovered, in Israel's response to God.[9]

The early Christian community likewise borrowed many of its moral teachings from the surrounding culture. Lists of virtues and vices as well as the famous household codes were taken over from the surrounding peoples. Paul explicitly talks about searching out the will of God (Rom. 12:1-2). Thus the will of God and morality are not proposed as revealed directly and immediately by God.[10] In his teaching on marriage, Paul proposes teachings in his own name and not teaching received from God. Thus even within the Scriptures themselves morality is proposed as something that is searched out and discovered by the community.

Much has been written in the last few decades about how Scripture is to be used in moral theology or Christian ethics. No one should be surprised at the variety and differences in the theories that have been proposed. However, the one common point in all these attempts is the recognition of the

---

[9]Sean Freyne, "The Bible and Christian Morality," in *Introduction to Christian Ethics: A Reader,* ed. Ronald P. Hamel and Kenneth R. Himes (New York: Paulist Press, 1989), 9–32.

[10]Victor Paul Furnish, *Theology and Ethics in Paul* (Nashville: Abingdon Press, 1968), 227–37. For Furnish's approach to discerning the will of God concerning homosexuality, see his "Understanding Homosexuality in the Bible's Cultural Particularity," *Circuit Rider* 15, 10 (December 1991–January 1992): 10–12.

insufficiency of Scripture for determining what is right and wrong in many issues facing our world today.

All who accept the role of tradition recognize this insufficiency. The church today cannot merely repeat the words of Scripture but must try to understand, live, and appropriate the word and work of Jesus in the light of the historical and cultural circumstances of the present. Many different theories explain what tradition is and how it functions, but the common element of all who give any role to tradition is the insufficiency of the Scriptures.[11]

Creeds form one of the practical manifestations of the acceptance of tradition. One of the signs of catholicity pointed out by Pelikan is the acceptance of creeds.[12] Many Christians today accept and use the Apostles' Creed and the Nicene-Constantinopolitan Creed. Many churches have developed later and even contemporary creedal formulations. The Reformed tradition of Protestantism recognizes a need for a frequent updating of its creeds.[13] Such a use of postscriptural creeds acknowledges the need for the living church to express its faith in words that are not derived immediately and directly from the Bible.

The role of tradition as a source of moral wisdom is also grounded in the understanding of the church in general and of catholicity in particular. The Holy Spirit animates the life of the church. In its catholicity the church exists in different times, places, and cultures. The living church under the in-

---

[11]See, for example, *Biblical Interpretation in Crisis: The Ratzinger Conference on Bible and Church,* ed. Richard John Neuhaus (Grand Rapids, Mich.: William B. Eerdmans, 1989).

[12]Pelikan, *Riddle of Catholicism,* 29, 30.

[13]*Creeds of the Churches: A Reader in Christian Doctrine from the Bible to the Present,* 3d ed., ed. John H. Leith (Atlanta: John Knox Press, 1982).

spiration of the Holy Spirit must become incarnate in the different times, places, and cultures in which it exists. Jesus has promised to the church the gift of the Holy Spirit to ensure that the church will always be faithful to the basic gospel message. But this fidelity includes the need to become living and incarnate in different times and places. The church catholic is called to creative fidelity as the community of the disciples of Jesus living in different times in history and in all parts of the globe. Many of the tensions experienced by the church come from its attempt to live out its creative fidelity to the word and work of Jesus. The living church under the inspiration of the Holy Spirit knows that creative fidelity strives to avoid the two extremes of fundamentalism and modernism. Fundamentalism merely repeats the words and formulations of the past. Modernism jettisons the core Christian realities in the light of the purported needs of the times.

In addition to Scripture and tradition, a catholic approach to morality gives some role to reason and human experience.[14] The catholic emphasis on embracing all cannot exclude human reason and experience from making some contribution to the moral wisdom and knowledge of the Christian community. Great differences exist about the meaning of human reason and experience, the different roles of reason and human experience, and how they relate to Scripture and tradition.

A number of theological warrants support the recognition of sources of moral wisdom that exist outside the explicit Christian community with its distinctive Christian sources of moral wisdom. Creation serves as a strong theological grounding for some acceptance of human reason and experience as sources of

[14]John Mahoney, *The Making of Moral Theology* (Oxford: Clarendon Press, 1987).

moral knowledge. God created the world, and it is good. God is present and acting in creation. The more radical sectarian approach sees sin as totally affecting and distorting creation so that what is created becomes identified with the sinful. Those in the catholic tradition who give a greater role to sin would see in the world of creation the preserving ordering of God at work.

The implications of the incarnation also support a more catholic understanding. In the incarnation the divine was joined with the human so that the human cannot be foreign to or opposed to the divine. The incarnation thus embraces and touches all the human. The catholic approach to salvation and redemption often recognizes that salvation takes place outside the confines of the Christian community itself. Many disputes exist about how and why this salvation occurs, but the catholic or universal aspect of the gift of salvation is recognized. Eschatology also sees the reign of God as affecting in some way the world and not just restricted to the confines of the church. A catholic ecclesiology does not identify the church with the reign of God, but sees the church as a sacrament or sign of the reign of God. (In this connection the contemporary Roman Catholic theologian Edward Schillebeeckx has insisted on the world as the place of salvation. Schillebeeckx, whose newest work on the church was written in response to some of the more recent authoritarian developments in Roman Catholicism, insists that whereas at one time Roman Catholicism maintained that outside the church there was no salvation, today one must recognize that outside the world there is no salvation. Not all would agree with Schillebeeckx, but his is one approach proposed today within the catholic and Roman Catholic communities that illustrates that salvation embraces more than just the church.)[15]

---

[15]Edward Schillebeeckx, *Church: The Human Story of God* (New

A catholic approach to Christian morality realizes the need to be in dialogue with all others outside the church and the possibility that the church might learn from such a dialogue. History reminds us that the churches in general have developed and even changed their moral positions in and through this broader dialogue. The approach of the Christian churches to slavery is not one of the more illustrious chapters in the history of Christian thinking about morality.[16] Most Christian churches changed their teaching in and through dialogue within and outside the church. The churches have also learned quite a bit from the culture in terms of the dignity and freedom of the human person. The churches themselves on their own did not come up with a strong justification of religious freedom. Religious intolerance has all too often been present in Christian churches. The existing recognition by the churches of human persons as free and actually called to participate in their own society owes much to a dialogue with the philosophy and political theory of the Enlightenment.[17] As will be mentioned later, the very fact that the Christian churches have learned from the Enlightenment but also have severely criticized aspects of it well illustrates the approach to morality from a catholic perspective within the churches themselves.

I have referred to two human sources of moral wisdom from which the catholic approach to morality can learn as reason and experience. The different understandings of reason and experience are legion and lie beyond the limits of the present discussion. These two are distinguished in this context for a number of reasons. Reason is often conceived in

---

York: Crossroad, 1991), 5–15.

[16] Maxwell, *Slavery in the Catholic Church.*

[17] *Religious Liberty and Human Rights in Nations and in Religions,* ed. Leonard Swidler (Philadelphia: Ecumenical Press, 1986).

a somewhat intellectual perspective, and the term *experience* opens up more intuitive and more completely human ways of knowing. Experience is singled out here to include especially the emphasis on concrete involvement proposed by many theories of praxis today. These two concepts are used in a catholic sense to include all ways of human knowing and are not meant to exclude any type of truly human knowing.

Thus a catholic approach to Christian morality recognizes that Christians can learn moral wisdom from non-Christian sources and persons. It lies beyond the scope of our considerations to talk about the limitations of non-Christian sources and persons as well as the effects of human sinfulness on them. Likewise no judgment will be made about the exact relationship of Christian and non-Christian sources of moral wisdom and knowledge.[18] The recognition that Christian morality can learn from sources and persons that are not explicitly Christian characterizes a catholic approach to Christian morality. Some will give a greater or lesser role to these sources, but the catholic characteristic is justified by recognizing that some things in the moral area can be learned from non-Christian sources and persons.

One practical illustration of a catholic theology in general and ethics in particular is the presence of Christian theology and ethics in the college or university. In the United States many denominational institutions of higher learning have a theology department. As an academic discipline, theology and theological ethics are in dialogue with the other disciplines on the campus. The existence of theology in just such a setting of higher education well illustrates the catholic nature

[18]For a recent debate in Roman Catholicism about what is unique or distinctive in Christian morality, see Vincent MacNamara, *Faith and Ethics: Recent Roman Catholicism* (Washington, D.C.: Georgetown University Press, 1985).

of the discipline and its need to be in dialogue with many other disciplines. A catholic theology is related not only to the church but also to the academy. Within the last few years tensions have arisen in a number of churches about the relationship between the church and the academy with regard to theology, but the very existence of theology within the academy illustrates the fact that theology can and must be in dialogue with the human arts and sciences.

The college or university setting for theology thus illustrates the catholic character of theological or Christian ethics. The systematic reflection on Christian morality is an academic discipline that must be in constant dialogue with other disciplines. Philosophy, sociology, psychology, literature, political science, history, and many other disciplines enter into the work of moral theology and Christian ethics, although, again, disputes abound as to how this is done.

Christian morality thus has many sources of wisdom and knowledge. If there were just one source, the approach to Christian morality would be much simpler, but it would not be catholic. There is no simple or easy way for the Christian church or the individual Christian to arrive at moral wisdom and knowledge. Such a catholic understanding definitely colors and influences the way in which the church arrives at its own understanding, teaching, and living of the moral life.

Different Levels of Morality

ANOTHER IMPORTANT PRESUPPOSITION BEFORE SKETCHING OUT the way in which the church teaches, lives, and bears witness to its moral life concerns the different levels of moral discourse. What is morality? What are the different aspects that make up morality? Here again a generic catholic approach opts for an inclusive rather than an exclusive attitude. At the very minimum morality involves more than merely discussing whether this particular act is right or wrong. A number of different aspects or elements can be distinguished in morality. I prefer to speak of these elements in a grid going from the more general to the more particular and specific. I hasten to add that not all will agree with the way in which I break down the different aspects of morality, but a truly catholic approach must include somewhat similar understandings.

The basic distinction in morality concerns the subject pole and the object pole of morality. Morality involves the person who acts and what that person does with its effect on others, society, and the world. Our consideration turns first to the subject pole of morality.

The most general aspect of the subject pole concerns the basic orientation of the person that influences all that the person thinks and does. Within the discipline of moral theology or Christian ethics there is no agreement about what to call or how to describe this basic orientation. Some, especially in the Lutheran tradition, have understood faith to be the basic response of the Christian to God's gift, and faith active in love constitutes the fundamental orientation or attitude of the disciples of Jesus.[19] Some have understood this basic attitude of the Christian in terms of love of God and neighbor with a love that radically involves the total commitment of the person and embraces all humankind, especially the persons most in need and the enemy.[20] Some refer to conversion—the basic change of heart by which the believer

[19]George Wolfgang Forell, *Faith Active in Love* (Minneapolis: Augsburg, 1959).

[20]Gene Outka, *Agape: An Ethical Analysis* (New Haven, Conn.: Yale University Press, 1972): see also Joseph L. Allen, *Love and Conflict: A Covenantal Model of Christian Ethics* (Nashville: Abingdon Press, 1984).

responds to the gift of God in Christ Jesus.[21] Discipleship has often been used to describe this fundamental orientation, but such a word has also been used especially in sectarian ways to describe the sectarian approach as distinguished from the more catholic approach to morality.[22] From a more philosophical perspective some have spoken about the fundamental option.[23] Different understandings have been proposed, but the important point of agreement involves the existence of a basic or fundamental orientation of the person that gives direction to one's moral life and actions.

In addition to the general orientation of the moral person, more specific virtues, attitudes, or dispositions greatly affect how one acts. The Christian Scriptures often mention different attitudes or virtues. Christians differ about the exact meaning of these attitudes, how they actually function, and how they are related among themselves; but at least catholic approaches to morality recognize the important role of these particular attitudes and dispositions that influence our actions.

My own personal preference is to explain the attitudes or virtues systematically in terms of the fundamental relationships of the Christian with God, neighbor, world, and self that characterize the Christian moral life. In the fundamental relationship to God, the basic disposition of the Christian, in my judgment, is an openness to hear and respond to the word

---

[21]Walter Conn, *Christian Conversion: A Developmental Interpretation of Autonomy and Surrender* (New York: Paulist Press, 1986).

[22]Stephen Happel and James J. Walter, *Conversion and Discipleship: A Christian Foundation for Ethics and Doctrine* (Philadelphia: Fortress Press, 1986).

[23]Josef Fuchs, "Basic Freedom and Morality," in *Introduction to Christian Ethics: A Reader,* ed. Hamel and Himes, 187–98.

and deed of God in Christ Jesus. Christian Scripture refers to such a disposition as being poor in spirit. Likewise thankfulness, gratitude, and worship will mark the life of one who believes that God has chosen and given us life and the fullness of life with no dependence on our works or accomplishments. Hope in the presence of God's continuing power and promise should also characterize the life of the disciple of Jesus. In terms of the relationship to neighbor, love, justice, compassion, forgiveness, and service should characterize the Christians.

Christians have traditionally talked about the attitude of stewardship that should affect our attitude toward the world and all of creation. Stewardship recognizes that the goods of creation exist to serve the needs of all God's people and that we must care for our ecosystem. Our relationship to ourselves must be guided by humility, honesty, and proper self-respect. In these sentences I have tried merely to indicate in a sketchy manner how the virtues could be understood without claiming to have developed a fully systematic approach. Although great differences abound in understanding the virtues or dispositions of the Christian moral life and how they function, all must recognize the important role that such attitudes play in the moral life of the Christian community and its members.

Intentionality and motivation constitute an important part of the moral reality with reference to the person as both subject and agent. Both theoretically and practically the question is often raised, Why be moral? Christian faith supplies not only a distinctive but also a unique motivation. Christians are to love one another as Jesus first loved us. Imitation of Jesus becomes a powerful motivating force for believers. Christian spirituality has frequently emphasized the need to make sure that everything Christians do and think comes from their Christian faith. Catholicity emphasizes a faith that permeates and touches everything.

The basic orientation, dispositions or virtues, and motivation refer primarily to the person as the subject pole of morality. But morality also involves the object pole, or, as I prefer to describe it, the multiple relations within which human beings exist—the relationships with God, neighbor, world, and self. Here too one can go from the general to the more specific level. I refer to the levels of values, principles, norms, and decision making that embody this move from the more general to the more specific in terms of the realities that affect the structures and institutions of human personal, social, political, cultural, and economic life.

An example of the values that should be sought and made real are justice and human rights. Here too a catholic approach attempts to be more inclusive in its approach to virtues. Justice and human rights are important values for society. Justice is an analogical concept embracing a number of different approaches depending on the relationships involved. A catholic concept of justice recognizes both unity and diversity with regard to the reality of justice and does not reduce all justice to one type. Commutative justice governs relationships involving one person with another, whereas distributive justice governs the relationship of the society and the state in distributing goods and burdens among the members of society. Social justice refers to the individual's relationship to society and government. The demands of justice are different in these different types. In an individualistic society the perennial danger consists in reducing all justice to the concept of commutative justice, which governs one-on-one relationships with the qualities of arithmetic equality and blindness to the persons involved. However, the distribution of the goods and burdens of society should not be determined by arithmetic equality. In distributing goods, those with basic human needs should have those basic human needs taken care of and met. In distributing burdens those who have more should contribute more.[24]

A catholic approach to human rights insists on both political and civil rights such as freedom of speech, religion, and assembly as well as social and economic rights such as rights to food, clothing, shelter, education, and health care. Our society in the United States tends to be too individualistic and thus emphasizes only the political and civil rights with their heavy emphasis on "freedom from." We as a society need to give greater recognition to social and economic rights that emphasize the "freedom for" aspect of our basic freedom.[25]

A specific value for society from the perspective of the church catholic concerns the need to include all, especially the poor, the marginalized, and the victims. In this context the preferential option for the poor and solidarity with victims comes to the fore.[26] The values on the object pole of moral consideration often correspond with the attitudes and virtues on the subject pole.

Principles are somewhat broad articulations of the directions in which human life should go. Once again a catholic perspective will influence one's understanding of the principles governing the moral life. In the realm of personal morality the catholic principle of the Golden Rule will come into play. In social morality the fundamental principle governing the just distribution of earthly goods insists that the goods of creation exist to serve the needs of all. The more concrete sys-

---

[24]Daniel C. Maguire, *A New American Justice: Ending the White Male Monopolies* (Garden City, N.Y.: Doubleday, 1980).
[25]David Hollenbach, *Justice, Peace, and Human Rights* (New York: Crossroad, 1988), 87–123.
[26]Lamb, *Solidarity with Victims.*

tems proposed for just distribution must be guided by this fundamental principle.

Norms are more specific than principles and more direct guides of human actions. Positive norms insist on what must be done. One must respect all other human beings; one must tell the truth. Negative norms prohibit actions such as lying, stealing, cheating. Heated discussions about the basis or grounding of norms and possible exceptions to them lie beyond this book.

The most concrete level of morality involves moral decision making that brings together the subject pole (the decision making of the person) and the object pole (the action that is to be done and that will affect our multiple relationships). The Christian tradition has generally discussed decision making under the rubric of conscience. Diverse theories and interpretations of conscience abound.[27] On the other hand all experience and recognize the basic dilemma of conscience: "I must follow my conscience, but my conscience might be wrong." This dilemma spurs the churches' continual concern about the formation of conscience.

A catholic approach must recognize these different dimensions of the moral life. Not all would agree with the terminology and distinctions mentioned here, but the multiple aspects and levels of the moral values cohere with a generic catholic approach. One important aspect of these diverse levels concerns the degree of generality and specificity involved. The more general the moral realities, the greater the area of agreement. For example, the general value of respect for human life can be accepted by all precisely because it is

[27]*Conscience: Theological and Psychological Perspectives,* ed. C. Ellis Nelson (New York: Newman Press, 1973).

general and contains little or no specific content. However, much disagreement exists within the Christian community about the death penalty or abortion. The more specific and concrete a matter becomes, the greater the area for disagreement among people who share the same basic values. Human reason and the testimony of the lived church experience today strongly support such a general understanding of the agreements and disagreements within and among the Christian churches.

The Discerning Church: A Catholic Community of Moral Discourse

THE PRELIMINARY CONSIDERATIONS OF THE DIFFERENT SOURCES of Christian morality and the different levels of moral realities prepare the way for discussing the internal moral life of the church. Our focus concerns how the church discerns and discovers its moral teaching and how it teaches or shares this in the formation of its own members. This section will concentrate on how the church discerns or discovers its moral teaching.

Chapter 1 mentioned many aspects of the churches' moral reality—a community of moral conviction, of moral doubt, and of moral practice; but the most fundamental reality concerns the church as a community of moral discourse. Through discourse the church discovers its convictions, doubts, and practices. As mentioned earlier, discourse should not be limited just to the intellectual and the theoretical realms. Discourse involves the total communication and sharing that takes place within the church community. Actions as well as thoughts constitute discourse. The thesis of this section contends that the church discerns and discovers its moral teaching by being a catholic and inclusive community of moral discourse.

The different sources of moral wisdom and knowledge for the church form part of its grounding as a community of moral discourse. No one source of moral wisdom is sufficient. Discourse or dialogue must exist among the various sources. The church itself constitutes the community of discourse, which then must ultimately decide its moral positions in the light of these different sources. The discerning church believes in the promise of Jesus that the Spirit will be present to assist the discernment process.

Whereas all who fit under the umbrella of the church catholic see the church community itself as deciding its own moral teaching, great differences exist about how each church goes about this discernment process. The Roman Catholic Church is probably the most structured, with its well-developed (and challenged) concept of a hierarchical teaching magisterium exercised by bishops in the church and in a special way by the bishop of Rome. Even Roman Catholicism, however, recognizes a role played by all members of the church in this moral discernment process. The so-called authoritative decision belongs to the hierarchical magisterium, but all the faithful have some contribution to make.[28] At its best the Roman Catholic tradition insisted on an intrinsic morality—something is commanded because it is good, and not the other way around. The will of authority does not determine morality according to the best insights of

[28]Ladislas Örsy, *The Church: Learning and Teaching* (Wilmington, Del.: Michael Glazier, 1987); Francis A. Sullivan, *Magisterium: Teaching Authority in the Catholic Church* (New York: Paulist Press, 1983).

the Roman Catholic tradition.[29] This understanding of morality coincides with the recognition that the hierarchical teaching office of the church is not above the word of God and truth but is in the service of the word of God and truth.[30]

From a catholic perspective many theological reasons support a role for all the people of God in discerning the moral life of the Christian community. The Holy Spirit is recognized as the primary teacher in the church, and the Spirit is given to all the individual members through baptism. The gift of the Spirit to all in the church serves as a basis for the *sensus fidelium.* History also shows how the various churches have learned from the lived experience of its members. In discerning its moral understanding, the whole church is a community of moral discourse in which all have some role to play.

The catholicity of moral discourse insists on an inclusive community of discourse. No one may be excluded from the dialogue and discussion. The catholic emphasis also underscores the fact that the church community needs to search out all available sources outside the church for what they can contribute to its understanding of morality.

History reminds us of the problems created by exclusive approaches. The greatest temptation for believers in general and Christians in particular is to make God into our own image and likeness. The Christian, like all other human beings, strives to find the strongest justification for one's actions; and for such a believer nothing can be stronger or more motivating than the support of God. A true catholicity strives to overcome the danger of individuals or particular groups using God, Jesus, and the gospel for their own purposes.

---

[29]Mahoney, *Making of Moral Theology,* 224–58.

[30]"Dogmatic Constitution on Divine Revelation," par. 10, *The Documents of Vatican II,* ed. Walter M. Abbott (New York: Guild Press, 1966), 118.

The catholicity of the church strives to overcome one of the inherent weaknesses in the moral decision-making process of any person or group. From a theological perspective, problems and errors in morality arise from two sources—finitude and sinfulness. Our finitude and contextualization mean that our perspective is always somewhat limited. From a purely ethical standpoint, one must always strive to compensate for the dangers arising from our limitations in time, space, history, and culture. The catholicity of the church serves as an effective antidote against the problems arising from our finitude. Apart from any ecclesiological consideration, the community of moral discourse in itself should also be catholic—striving to include all and exclude none.

Even within the church catholic the temptation of exclusion is often present. Individual local communities will never be fully catholic in reality. Most local communities need to become more catholic and more inclusive than they are. The local community can never forget that it is part of the broader and more inclusive church and is always challenged to strive for a full catholicity in spirit. The church can never succumb to the temptation of being a club of like-minded persons. The local church needs to transcend its own limitations to have a more catholic horizon. The marginalized and the poor in society cannot be forgotten and put out of sight and out of consideration. The local church cannot become a place of refuge from the problems of the wider society. A catholic approach strives to include all, both within and outside the church, in its moral discourse.

Moral Unity and Diversity

THE THIRD CRITERION OF CATHOLICITY ACCEPTED IN THESE PAGES concerns unity and diversity. Catholicity cannot become uniformity. The primary Christian concepts of the Trinity, with its unity of the three divine persons, and the incarnation, with the union in Jesus of the divine and the human, exemplify this unity in diversity. The inherent tensions in the understanding of catholicity are very evident. The goal of true catholicity remains elusive for the believing community; full catholicity has never been achieved. On the one hand uniformity can readily replace unity. Uniformity does away with legitimate diversity in the overzealous attempt to ensure catholicity. On the other hand divisions and exclusive emphases too readily destroy the unity and catholicity of the church. At times divisions have often occurred in reaction to a one-sided uniformity.

All three characteristics of catholicity—open to include all persons, embracing all reality, and maintaining diversity in the midst of unity—come to bear on this question of the unity and diversity of the church, whether local, regional, national, or universal, with regard to morality and moral issues. History reminds us in general how impossible it is to achieve full catholicity. Catholicity has probably been the most contentious issue in the history of Christianity and of particular churches. Most of the pages of church history abound with the tensions of catholicity because much of church history has focused primarily on the institutions and their lives. History also reminds us, however, that most of the tensions in catholicity have not centered on moral issues. The primary concerns have been doctrinal or disciplinary. The creeds proposed by the churches both in ancient times and in modern times generally say little or nothing about morality. Since creeds often arise in response to particular challenges and problems, one can conclude that moral issues did not constitute the primary problems or tensions facing the church's catholicity.

Ecumenical dialogue and discussions historically have not seen moral issues as sources of division between the churches. In the contemporary scene in the United States the bilateral dialogue between Lutherans and Roman Catholics stands out as the most significant and productive of all the existing dialogues. This dialogue considered all the outstanding divisive issues such as justification, sanctification, Scripture and tradition, the Eucharist, ministry, authority, the Petrine office and infallibility, and Mary and the saints. The dialogue never once considered a specific moral issue. Apparently, in the eyes of this important group, moral issues do not constitute a source of division between the churches.

Yet sometimes moral issues have been involved in the tensions of catholicity. The churches' divisions over slavery during the American Civil War furnish a good example. At the present time many churches remain divided over issues that arose at the time of the Civil War.[31] Today many of our individual churches experience great tensions over issues of sexuality. Perhaps the American penchant for the pragmatic and the concrete has been at work in this country.

Why historically have moral issues not been a source of division between the churches? A number of possible explanations come to mind. Before the present century the Christian world tended to be much more culturally homogeneous. Generally speaking, agreement existed on all sorts of moral issues, including the condemnation of contraception for married people. In such culturally homogeneous settings, moral disagreement did not come to the fore to be a divisive force between the churches.

Another possible explanation comes from the fact that

---

[31]Goen, *Broken Churches.*

churches and theologians insisted much more on orthodoxy and gave much less concern to orthopraxis. A greater emphasis on the role of moral practice today might make moral issues more central in considerations of catholicity.

These two reasons may have contributed to the fact that specific moral issues did not constitute a source of division between churches, but I still think a distinctive characteristic of morality at least implicitly influenced the lack of division over specific moral issues.

The basic criterion of catholicity with its acceptance of unity and diversity in the context of embracing all persons and realities distinguishes between what is core to the faith and what is more peripheral. Catholic faith touches all the different aspects of life but recognizes that some realities are more central than others. Down through the centuries the various creeds have tried to enumerate the core or basic teachings of the church in general or in one of the individual churches.

The distinction between what is core and what is more peripheral or removed from the core is very important for a proper functioning of catholicity. Agreement and unity must exist on the level of what is pivotal and necessary for one to belong to the community of the disciples of Jesus. This community stands for something; not all can or even want to be members and to accept what it means to belong to this community. History reminds of the travails and difficulties in trying to determine the basic constituents of membership in the church. Divisive moral matters, however, have generally not occasioned divisions and breakoffs within the Christian churches.

Why has the basic criterion of catholicity distinguishing between what is core and what is more peripheral been easier to apply in moral matters? At least implicitly two distinctive characteristics of morality have been functioning here as added criteria to better explain the distinction between what is core and what is peripheral.

The first ethical criterion recognizes the distinction between more general moral affirmations and more particular moral affirmations. On the more general level, greater universality and agreement exist. As realities become more specific and complex, the level of universality and agreement definitely recedes. The logic of catholicity's unity in diversity recognizes the need for this distinction between the level of the more general or universal and the level of the more specific and the particular.

In the past and at present Christians within the same church have disagreed about many moral issues. The Christian Scriptures contain references to differences within the early Christian community about sharing goods in common, marriage and remarriage, relationships with others outside the Christian community. In the life of the early church questions and diverse practices existed with regard to involvement in certain civil and cultural practices, the meaning and practice of marriage and sexuality, and the use of force and violence. Today our churches experience diversity in many moral areas. Recall the discussion over the United States' military involvement in Vietnam, Panama, Grenada, and the recent Persian Gulf War. Heated debates have occurred among and within the churches over abortion and homosexuality.

At the same time, however, the Christian churches from the very beginning have experienced in theory and practice agreement and unity in more general areas of moral response. All accept the necessity and importance of faith, conversion, and discipleship even though each individual may have a different interpretation of how these realities are to be understood, developed, and lived out. Agreement about these general moral perspectives and responses has existed in the past and continues to exist today. Too often people fail to recognize the area of agreement that exists in the ambience of the church in the midst of the many sharp disagreements surrounding particular issues. Such general agreement should not be dismissed as merely platitudinous and inconsequential. General perspectives and attitudes do give a direction and shape to the life of the Christian community and should influence all the particular decisions we make and actions we do. In the creeds and controversies about unity and catholicity throughout the centuries, it was simply assumed, I believe, that agreement existed on these general moral perspectives. Since there was no division over these realities, there was no pressing need to include them as part of the creeds, which often arose in the early church to settle disputed questions.

In principle and in practice this distinction between the more general moral realities and the more specific ones has at least been implicitly recognized and practiced in recent history by many different Christian churches. In a sense the distinction between the more general and the more specific is easy to understand and accept. Problems arise in the gray area that exists between the two. Especially as one gives more content to the general understanding, one becomes more specific and recognizes the possibility of disagreement and divergence within the Christian community. The sound criterion of catholicity recognizes that the more specific and concrete the reality, the more pluralism and diversity will exist.

A second ethical criterion for guidance in distinguishing between what is core and what is peripheral concerns the distinction between negative and positive moral judgments. It is easier to find agreement that something is wrong than it is to say what positively should be done to overcome the wrong. In a certain sense the Ten Commandments illustrate this reality. They are stated negatively but also are formal and general. The Christian churches have traditionally recognized the Decalogue while accepting different interpretations on complex and specific areas. (It should be pointed out that while all the mainline Christian churches accept the Decalogue, there exist different ways of enumerating it.) A negative command marks off certain actions as wrong but leaves open a great area of options for what might positively be done. Thus at times within churches it will be easier to agree on what should not be done than it will be to agree on what positively should be done. All Christians, for example, agree that one should not worship false gods, but Christians disagree about how the true God is best worshiped. General agreement exists in the United States today about the inadequacy of our health care system, but the country cannot agree on what should be done to change the present system.

These criteria can now be applied to the different sources of morality and the different levels of moral reality discussed in the first part of this chapter. With regard to the different sources of morality, only the one question of the role of Scripture in determining Christian morality will be mentioned. The use of Scripture in moral theology is a perennial question that has received quite a bit of attention in the last few years. A nonfundamentalistic understanding of the Scriptures recognizes that the scriptural witness is incarnated in a particular historical, cultural, and social framework that differs from our own. The differing historical and cultural situations will have a much greater impact on the more specific and complex moral issues than on the more general aspects of morality. Thus, for example, all can agree that the biblical concepts of mercy and forgiveness should characterize the Christian person today. However, the biblical attitude toward women might not be appropriate in our contemporary circumstances. In the light of the criteria discussed here, one can and should expect to find unity within the Christian community on those things that are core to faith and more general. The Scriptures themselves in relationship to morality will play a much more direct role in these areas than in the more complex and specific moral issues.[32] Although I briefly mention the use of Scripture in Christian ethics here because it has been receiving so much attention recently, the primary concern in this section involves the different levels of the moral reality.[33]

All Christians should agree about the general orientation of the Christian moral life, but this general reality is explained and developed in different ways—for example, faith, conversion, discipleship, love of God and neighbor. Likewise general conformity and agreement exist in the Christian church and tradition on the attitudes, virtues, or dispositions that should characterize the Christian life even though there are different theological and philosophical understandings of how these attitudes are rooted in the acting person and how they influence human actions. Christians have traditionally shared and stressed the importance of faith, hope, and love as fundamental virtues. Gratitude, openness to God's loving gifts, compassion for the neighbor, concern for the poor, a love that strives to be inclusive rather than exclusive, and a special care for those most in need illustrate the attitudes that should be accepted in general by all Christians. The Christian community and its members will also share the same basic Christian motivation. Likewise in terms of the object pole of Christian morality, agreement exists on the general values of justice, respect for persons, fairness, hon-

[32]This conclusion is also maintained by Rasmussen and Birch, *Bible and Christian Ethics.*

[33]For other approaches, see *Readings in Moral Theology No. 4: The Use of Scripture in Moral Theology,* ed. Charles E. Curran and Richard A. McCormick (New York: Paulist Press, 1984).

esty, and care for those in need as values that should be present in our churches and in our world.

Both historically and in the contemporary context disagreements have arisen about the morality of particular moral judgments and especially about the morality of quite specific norms. General norms, such as showing respect for a human person, can readily be admitted by all. Formal norms involve no material dimensions and therefore can generally be accepted by all. Thus, for example, the Christian tradition agrees that murder is always wrong, since murder is really unjustified killing. In some cases, however, the Christian tradition has generally been willing to admit that killing is acceptable. Killing is a material term that embraces a very specific type of action. Even though this action generally might be wrong, one can think of circumstances in which it might be acceptable.

The basic criterion is clear. As one moves from what is core to what is more remote and from what is more general to what is more specific, the possibility of legitimate diversity within the church catholic arises. The extremes, as always, are evident. All Christians must recognize the importance and need of conversion, but Christians legitimately disagree about the death penalty in human society. The primary area of dispute concerns the more specific moral norms. In this and in similar disputes, casuistry is helpful in clarifying what is at stake.

The Christian tradition has held that adultery is wrong. Strong scriptural and traditional warrants exist for this condemnation. The experience of the Christian community today indicates a general strong support for the immorality of adultery. Reason points out the manifold bases for the condemnation of adultery, which involves an injury to one's spouse, a violation of one's own marriage commitment, and deleterious effects on the important institution of marriage itself. In very unusual circumstances, such as Joseph Fletcher's famous case of Mrs. Bergmeier, one might excuse or even justify adultery. According to Joseph Fletcher's case, Mrs. Bergmeier was imprisoned in a Soviet camp after the war and prevented from returning to her husband and family in Germany. She discovered, however, that if she were pregnant she would be released from the prison and allowed to go home. She seduced the guard, became pregnant, was released from prison, and had a joyful homecoming with her family in Germany.[34] For the reasons mentioned, however, the general condemnation of adultery brings out a unanimous judgment within the Christian community.

The Christian churches in South Africa recently faced the issue of apartheid. For a long time the Dutch Reformed Church accepted and even defended the practice of apartheid. Other predominantly white churches slowly came to a condemnation of apartheid. Some churches, such as the Lutheran and the Reformed, strongly affirmed that the acceptance of apartheid was incompatible with membership in the community of the disciples of Jesus. I firmly agree with this latter judgment. Casuistry helps to clarify why apartheid is incompatible with what is core in the Christian belief. Apartheid directly and immediately violates the equal dignity and respect due to all human beings. One might respond that apartheid did not directly attack basic human equality, since it called for separate development of the different races in South Africa. However, in that situation and in the manner in which it was done, apartheid practically denied the basic equality of all human beings and reduced nonwhites to the level of second-class citizens who in no way could fully participate in deter-

[34]Joseph Fletcher, *Situation Ethics: The New Morality* (Philadelphia: Westminster Press, 1966), 164, 165.

mining their human and political situation. Also note the negative nature of this judgment. Those who share the negative conclusion about apartheid did not and could not agree on how to dismantle apartheid and what system to put in its place.[35]

Within the churches today intense debate and often acrimonious discussions have taken place on issues such as homosexuality, abortion, and euthanasia. In all likelihood debate on these issues will continue within many churches. I believe that pluralism and disagreements on this level as illustrated by these issues are appropriate within the church catholic. Here we find examples of concrete issues that are far removed from the core of faith and involve a degree of complexity and specificity that renders absolute certitude impossible. On the issue of abortion the primary question from a logical perspective concerns the status of the fetus. If the status is a truly individual human being, then it should be treated as such. Yet the judgment about the nature of the fetus is so complex that one cannot claim a certitude that excludes the possibility of error in determining what it is. Genetics, medicine, and biology are not going to be able to solve the human question of the status of the fetus. A human judgment is required that takes into account all the relevant data. People who share faith in Jesus Christ and live in the same Christian community of the church can and will disagree about the judgment of the nature of the fetus.

Homosexuality has become a hotly disputed question in many churches today. Again, such disputes from within a catholic perspective are to be accepted and recognized as legitimate. Some have argued that the condemnation of homo-

---

[35] *Apartheid Is a Heresy,* ed. John W. deGruchy and Charles Villa-Vicencio (Grand Rapids, Mich.: William B. Eerdmans, 1983).

sexual acts is clear from Scripture and from the tradition and history of the Christian churches. However, the historical and cultural context may very well have changed. Today we know more about the psychological phenomenon of constitutional or irreversible homosexuality. Is the person with such a constitution called to a celibate life? One can at least see why there is discussion about this issue today. The biblical authors did not know as much about the psychological aspects of sexual orientation as we know today. However, I do not think that the Christian tradition has nothing to contribute to the present debate, nor should any type of homosexual acts be sanctioned. Christians in general can agree that sexual relationships must take place within a context of personal commitment, and the consensual aspect of sexuality must always be highlighted.

The recent debates about euthanasia will, I believe, become more prominent both inside and outside the churches in the foreseeable future. Here too the issue is removed from the core of faith and involves matters that are far from certain. Within the catholic church general agreement exists that one does not have to do everything possible to keep human life in existence. The tradition has generally condemned suicide and euthanasia on the basis of the fact that we human beings do not have full control or dominion over our lives. But how much control and dominion do we have? Believing Christians could come to the conclusion that euthanasia in some circumstances might not be wrong. Yet Christians can never accept a purely utilitarian view of human life, deny the redemptive aspects of suffering, nor forget that life is God's gift. There is room for such disagreement on specifics within the church catholic precisely because of the complex matter involved and the fact that such issues are far removed from the core of faith.

In these areas of moral disagreement and doubt, the church as a community of moral discourse continues to have an important role to play. Concern for moral truth should characterize the whole church and the individual members of the church. Honest dialogue can and should occur within the church. The legitimacy of differences within the ecclesial community should not support a flabby moral pluralism. The search for moral truth remains an important imperative for the church as a whole and for the individual Christian. Church members should honestly grapple with disputed issues and be open to the truth wherever they might find it. I hold somewhat conservative positions on abortion and euthanasia and am willing to defend these postions in all forums and, above all, in the church.

Church as Moral Teacher

THE CHURCH NOT ONLY LEARNS WITH REGARD TO MORALITY BUT also teaches morality. Christians are obligated to respond in word and deed to the call of God in Jesus through the Spirit. The church forms and nourishes the faith and life of its members. Here too a catholic approach recognizes not only the different levels of morality but also the many different ways in which moral teaching and formation occur. The whole community of the church has a role to play in the moral formation of its members. All churches have professional ministers dealing with education and formation, but each baptized Christian has a teaching function not only in one's own moral formation but also in the moral formation of others and of the entire church community.

Word and sacrament are important sources of moral formation in the community, especially with regard to the general orientation of the moral life, the virtues or dispositions of the person, and the values that should be present in our relationships with one another. Those churches that emphasize the liturgical aspect should appreciate more the connection between liturgy and morality, especially with regard to the moral formation of the members of the community.[36]

One of the forgotten aspects of morality involves the moral imagination.[37] The Christian community needs to engage and fire the moral imagination of its members. The Christian story as made present in word and sacrament has the most significant role to play in the moral formation of the baptized. The whole community shares and participates in this story and tries to make this story their own. The lives of the heroines and the heroes of the community can also inspire people today. These saints have an important role to play in providing inspiration and examples to the other members of the community. The liturgy, the imaginative portrayal of the moral life, the example of heroic figures, and the mutual support of the members of the community constitute important ways in which the church carries out its moral teaching and formation.

Also important is the oral and written handing down of moral advice, aphorisms, principles, and norms. Too often the teaching of morality is reduced merely to the proposal of specific norms of conduct. In reality such an approach should constitute a comparatively small part of the total role of the church as a moral teacher. Morality involves more than rules or aphorisms, and teaching involves more than just inculcating these norms.

---

[36]"Focus on Liturgy and Ethics," *The Journal of Religious Ethics* 7 (Fall 1979): 139–249. This focus includes articles by Paul Ramsey, D. E. Sailers, Margaret A. Farley, William W. Everett, Martin D. Yaffe, Ronald M. Green, and Phillip J. Rossi.

[37]Philip S. Keane, *Christian Ethics and Imagination* (New York: Paulist Press, 1984).

Most church people today recognize the problem and the challenge in passing on the faith tradition and all that implies to the next generation. There are no easy answers to the challenge, but the church community must use better and more imaginatively all the educational resources it has at its disposal. Especially in moral formation and teaching the church has to compete with many other sources of teaching and influence that can very readily be opposed to its own ethos and understanding.

In teaching morality the whole church must also recognize the different levels of unity and pluralism or disagreement that can exist within the church. Gray areas will always exist, and tensions will surround these gray areas. However, history reminds us that the church has continuously experienced such tensions and disagreements.

In conclusion, the living church is a community of moral discourse in which all the members of the community have something to contribute in the broadest possible dialogue, learning from the sources of Scripture, tradition, reason, and experience. The catholicity of the church calls for agreement on those moral realities that are more central and core to faith and more general and formal. Disagreement and differences are to be expected on aspects that are more removed from the core of faith and are more complex and specific involving some very concrete norms, judgments of an individual nature, or the application of principles in different situations. The churches will always know the tension of dealing with specific and complex moral issues.

The church catholic will try to involve all its members in many different ways to teach all the different levels and aspects of morality to the church. All in the church catholic are truly teachers as well as learners.

CHAPTER 3

Catholicity and the Church's Moral Involvement in Society

THE CHURCH CATHOLIC RECOGNIZES THAT GOD AND JESUS, AS well as the church inspired by the Holy Spirit, have a concern for all aspects of human life in this world. The faith of the church catholic embraces all reality. The doctrine of creation forms an important grounding for such an understanding. In addition to creation the incarnation reminds us that the divine has touched all the aspects of the human.

Likewise a catholic approach recognizes that God's grace exists even beyond the explicit boundaries of the Christian church. H. Richard Niebuhr, in his classic *Christ and Culture*, acknowledged that all mainstream churches accept some relationship between Christ and culture and a Christian concern for what takes place in culture.[1] Some Christians today stress that the saving activity of God is directed primarily to the world, for the reign of God ultimately embraces all creation.[2]

The basic Christian realities of sin and grace have a social and cosmic dimension to them. Sin, for example, as detailed

[1] H. Richard Niebuhr, *Christ and Culture* (New York: Harper Torchbooks, 1956).
[2] Schillebeeckx, *Church,* 5–15.

in Genesis affects not only human relationships to God but also the relationships of one to another and to the world. Note how sin affected Adam and Eve's relationship to each other. The two were to become one flesh, but after their sin Adam pointed an accusing finger at Eve—she did it, not me. And then their son killed his brother. In the worldview of the authors of Genesis, the man is affected in what is understood to be the primary activity of work, whereas the woman experiences the effects of sin in the difficulties and pains of childbirth. The cosmic aspect of sin is seen in its growing power and effect in the whole world.

The social, public, and political aspects of the gospel message have been developed especially in a number of different theologies. The social gospel school in the United States at the turn of the century had a lasting effect on American churches.[3] Liberation theology, which began in Latin America in the late 1960s, has spread its influence throughout the world.[4] Black theology and feminist theology strongly resist the privatization of faith and the gospel.[5]

The social mission of the church involves a concern for and a mission to the justice and peace of the human community. However, the precise way in which the relationship between the church and the world is understood and structured differs considerably even within the same churches.

---

[3] *The Social Gospel in America, 1870–1920,* ed. Robert T. Handy (New York: Oxford University Press, 1966).

[4] Gustavo Gutiérrez, *A Theology of Liberation,* 15th anniversary ed. (Maryknoll, N.Y.: Orbis Books, 1988).

[5] James H. Cone, *Black Theology and Black Power,* 20th anniversary ed. (San Francisco: Harper & Row, 1989); Letty M. Russell, *Human Liberation in a Feminist Perspective* (Philadelphia: Westminster Press, 1974).

Privatization of Faith and the Gospel

ALTHOUGH THE CHURCH CATHOLIC BY DEFINITION HAS A CONcern for life in all its dimensions in the world, many churches have experienced the danger of privatization, which restricts the church and its role to the sphere of the personal, the private, the individual, and the familial. The American cultural and political scene have had some influence on the privatization of religion in general and of Christianity in particular.

From a cultural perspective the great influence of the professions and the sciences seems to have replaced the role of religion. Legal matters belong to lawyers; economic questions to economists; medical questions to doctors. Fortunately our society today is questioning many of these assumptions. Some purely technical issues are the exclusive province of the profession or science involved, but many issues, problems, or questions are not just legal, economic, or medical. Whatever affects human persons, human communities, and their environment is by that very nature a human issue, a moral issue, and of concern to the believing Christian individual and community. Questions such as tax rates and unemployment rates are not just economic issues. Although they involve much economic data, such issues are truly human and moral and, for the believer, Christian issues.

The basic catholic approach sees faith as touching and embracing all aspects of life. No truly human aspect can ever exist apart from faith. The fact that Christian faith touches all these matters does not mean that there is a ready-made Christian solution to all these problems. Catholic faith involves all aspects of the human. The human itself is catholic and broader than the dimensions of any one science—physical, social, or human. The broad human perspective at times must say no to what seems good from the viewpoint of a particular individual science. Sociology, for instance, might add to its store of knowledge through some experiments that infringe on the rights of individuals. Every human science is particular and partial in relationship to the fully human, and sometimes the truly human perspective must say no to what seems good from the perspective of one science.

In the United States another factor has influenced the popular conception that religion and politics or the public order should never mix. To its credit the United States has recognized the separation of church and state and incorporated this in the First Amendment. I am not advocating the union of church and state. But the separation of church and state should not mean the privatization of religion in general and Christianity in particular. The separation of church and state was never meant to imply the separation of religion or church and society.[6] Religion and churches have something to contribute to a more just, free, participative, and sustainable world.[7] A faith perspective should influence all that we do.

More specifically from the viewpoint of Christian churches, the Christian faith should influence and affect one's understanding of the commonweal and the public good of human society. Concern for the proper distribution of human goods and for protecting and enhancing the human rights of

---

[6]For a helpful overview that seems somewhat too critical of mainstream Protestant churches, see A. James Reichley, *Religion in American Public Life* (Washington: Brookings Institute, 1985).

[7]For a criticism of individualism in the United States and an insistence on the role of biblical communitarianism, see Robert N. Bellah et al., *Habits of the Heart: Individualism and Commitment in American Life* (Berkeley: University of California Press, 1985); Bellah et al., *The Good Society* (New York: Alfred A. Knopf, 1991).

all can and should be based on one's Christian faith. However, here too the catholic principles shape our understanding. As one moves from the general to the more complex and specific, there will be room for greater disagreements and more pluralism in the church and among its members. All can agree that society should have a concern for the poor, but differences will exist on the concrete means of enfleshing that vision and the ways to bring it about. Most catholic Christians recognize that the nations of the world today are not called to total pacifism. The use of military force cannot be ruled out as a possibility in some situations. People who share this perspective, however, will often disagree about the justification of using military force in a particular situation.

From the viewpoint of the First Amendment to the Constitution, some limits as well as freedoms exist with regard to the role of the churches.[8] History reminds us that the churches and church members have exerted influence on society in many different ways. Civil rights stands out as illustrating the role of churches and individual church members in working for social change. Today the involvement of the churches in the abortion issue specifically on behalf of the

[8]In addition to Marty and Reichley, see Robert Booth Fowler, *Religion and Politics in America* (Metuchen, N.J.: The American Theological Library Association and the Scarecrow Press, 1985), and Christopher F. Mooney, *Public Virtue: Law and the Social Character of Religion* (Notre Dame, Ind.: University of Notre Dame Press, 1986). From my perspective the most helpful recent work on the subject is Richard P. McBrien, *Caesar's Coin: Religion and Politics in America* (New York: Macmillan, 1987). McBrien writes from a Roman Catholic perspective proposing a middle position between those of absolute separationism and neoconservatism while studying in detail the Roman Catholic Church's involvement in the abortion issue.

pro-life position has created quite a bit of discussion and acrimony within the body politic.[9] All agree (it is always easier in hindsight) that some past involvement by churches has been inappropriate. One example was the Protestant churches' involvement in bringing about Prohibition. Another was the efforts of the Roman Catholic Church to keep on the books laws prohibiting the sale and use of contraception.[10]

From the viewpoint of the First Amendment, one can and must distinguish proper involvement of the churches in the political order from improper involvement.[11] But what are the criteria for determining what is proper? The Supreme Court has ruled that among other things the matter in question (e.g., the proposed law) must have a truly secular purpose.[12] I agree with what I think is the substance of this position, but I disagree with the terminology. The word *secular* is often used as opposed to religious. Thus secularism is looked upon as the enemy of religion. I prefer the word *political* purpose rather than *secular* purpose. *Political* is here understood in the classical sense of the *polis*, the city or the political society. Proposed legislation or public policy must have a truly political purpose. The controlling criterion is the purpose and not the motivation, or the basis, or sources used

---

[9]*The Catholic Church and Abortion Politics: A View from the States,* ed. Timothy A. Byrnes and Mary C. Segers (Boulder, Colo.: Westview Press, 1992).

[10]Norman St. John Stevas, *Birth Control and Public Policy* (Santa Barbara, Calif.: Center for the Study of Democratic Institutions, 1960).

[11]For an overview of the cases and decisions of the Supreme Court, see McBrien, *Caesar's Coin,* 53–91; Reichley, *Religion in American Public Life,* 115–67.

[12]*Committee for Public Education V. Nyquist,* 413 U.S. 756, 773 (1973).

in coming to one's conclusions. In the civil rights movement, for instance, the churches played a rather significant role in changing American policy and legislation. Yet many non-Christians and nonbelievers also participated in the same struggle and perhaps were even more influential. The determining criterion is not the motivation, the reasons, or the grounding of one's proposed policy or legislation but its purpose.

As another example let us consider briefly the involvement of the Roman Catholic Church in the United States in the abortion issue.[13] The Roman Catholic bishops, speaking for the whole church, have committed themselves and their church to work for a pro-life position and to overturn the *Roe v. Wade* decision of the Supreme Court.[14] How should one evaluate such an involvement?

Many have accused the American Roman Catholic bishops of violating the First Amendment and trying to foist their religious perspectives on others. I disagree. All should admit that the defense of human rights is a truly political purpose. If one believes that the fetus is a truly human being, then from the viewpoint of the role of the church and the believer in a pluralistic society, one has every right to work for a law to protect that human life. Defense of human life constitutes a truly political purpose. The leadership of the Roman Catholic Church must try to convince their fellow citizens of the truth of their position. Those who disagree with the American Roman Catholic bishops should not accuse them of violating

[13]For an understanding of the debate within Roman Catholicism, see *Abortion and Catholicism: The American Debate,* ed. Patricia Beattie Jung and Thomas A. Shannon (New York: Crossroad, 1988).
[14]Mary C. Segers, "The Bishops, Birth Control, and Abortion Policy: 1950–1985," in *Church Polity and American Politics: Issues in Contemporary American Catholicism,* ed. Mary C. Segers (New York: Garland, 1990).

the separation of church and state. Any individual or group in the United States has the right to work for legislation to defend basic human rights.

Disagreement, however, is perfectly in order, but such disagreement should go to the heart of the matter. The people who disagree with the position taken by the American Roman Catholic bishops disagree with the fundamental presupposition that the fetus, especially in its early stages, is a truly individual human life deserving the protections of a human person in our society. Religious groups in particular should avoid charging the Roman Catholic bishops with violating the First Amendment, for such a charge could boomerang to prevent the churches from dealing with truly political issues in the future. The abortion debate has created more heat than light, and the rhetoric at times has been appalling. The danger in all these heated issues is to use whatever arguments one can against an opponent. However, one must be careful and precise. Those who disagree with the American Roman Catholic bishops should disagree on the basic assumption of when truly individual human life begins and not resort to charging them with infringing on the separation of church and state.

From the perspective of how a catholic church should approach these issues, I disagree with the American Roman Catholic bishops. The issue of abortion law is very specific and complex. The Roman Catholic tradition itself has recognized the complexity by insisting on the difference between morality and legality. In practice some bishops often act as if no Catholic can be in favor of the present legal arrangement about abortion in the United States.[15] I believe this is a very

[15]Peter Augustine Lawler, "The Bishops versus Cuomo," in *Church Polity and American Politics,* ed. Segers, 175–93.

concrete and complex issue in which people who share the same faith can come down on different sides of the issue for different reasons.[16] Again, the abortion issue seems to be so heated that it occasions poor ethical and moral discourse. In their treatment of nuclear use and deterrence as well as in their teaching on the United States economy, the United States Roman Catholic bishops have clearly pointed out that there can be diversity within the church on matters of particular judgments in complex situations and in the application of principles to particular cases.[17] Such a realization also logically applies to abortion legislation.

The particular question of abortion raises the broader issue of what are appropriate matters for law and public policy in our country. The proposed legislation must have a political purpose. But how does one determine what is a truly political purpose? Disagreement exists on this point, but I propose the following criteria. In American society the basic principle of jurisprudence insists that the benefit of the doubt should be given to the freedom of the individual. The states or government should intervene with coercion only for the defense of the public good or the public order. The public order involves an order of justice and social justice, an order of public morality, and an order of peace.[18]

American jurisprudence illustrates the application of

---

[16]For a further explanation of my position, see my *Transition and Tradition in Moral Theology* (Notre Dame, Ind.: University of Notre Dame Press, 1979), 207–50.

[17]National Conference of Catholic Bishops, *Economic Justice for All: Pastoral Letter on Catholic Social Teaching and the U.S. Economy* (Washington, D.C.: United States Catholic Conference, 1986), nn. 134, 135, p. 68.

[18]I am proposing here with some modification the position of John Courtney Murray. See my *Directions in Catholic Social Ethics* (Notre Dame, Ind.: University of Notre Dame Press, 1985), 130–33.

these criteria. Consider the restrictions that have been placed on the free exercise of religion in the United States. All agree that the government can step in to prevent human sacrifice even in the context of religious worship, for one of the primary functions of government is the protection of human rights, especially the right to life. The aspect of morality in these criteria refers to public morality, not private morality. Recall, for example, that our society prevented Mormons from practicing polygamy, which was one of the tenets of their religion. The Supreme Court judged that such a practice was opposed to public morality. Likewise even religions cannot disturb the public peace, so that a religious procession involving a two-hundred-piece band walking around a residential neighborhood at three in the morning can rightly be prohibited. These three criteria of justice and social justice, public morality, and public peace provide the basis for determining what is a truly political purpose. Gray areas will continue to exist, but these criteria help to sort out the existing problems. For example, they would exclude public compulsory prayer to God and the erection of religious symbols on public property. These actions do not have a truly political purpose.

In addition, other pragmatic considerations are required to determine if something should be a law. Laws must be enforceable. If a law cannot be enforced, it should not be a law. Likewise laws must be fair to all and not discriminate against some. In the making of law, feasibility plays a very significant role. Many are willing to admit that at times half a loaf is better than none. Lawmaking involves the compromises of human political wisdom. Very often people will be willing to accept a partial gain of what they want rather than have nothing.

Such criteria can and should guide the churches and individuals in their attempt to safeguard and bring about a free, just, participative, and sustainable society. The very complexity of the criteria also reminds us that on specific issues there will usually be room for disagreement among people who share the same faith. Note the word *usually*. At times I think Christian faith might require acceptance of a particular issue and action by those who are members of the church. The last chapter pointed out that some Christians and churches in South Africa rightly insisted that opposition to apartheid was a demand of Christian faith.[19] Here again note the negative character of that judgment. Christians have to be opposed to apartheid. However, there is no universal agreement among Christians about the particular steps to be taken to overcome apartheid.

Religious faith should have some impact and influence on the broader human society. Churches too should have some role to play in this area. The catholic tradition cannot accept the claim that political, legal, and economic matters are totally independent of religious and ethical consideration. Both the criteria derived from catholicity and the criteria derived from the understanding of the First Amendment in our religiously pluralistic society guide and direct what are proper involvements.

The Broad Areas of Church Involvement Today

SPECIFIC ISSUES ARE IMPORTANT REALITIES, BUT, AS POINTED OUT in chapter 2, they constitute only one small part of morality and the aspects of morality. In considerations of society, however, this level takes on added significance because of the need and importance of structures in society. Social change

[19] *Apartheid Is a Heresy,* ed. deGruchy and Villa-Vicencio.

and social justice cannot occur without the necessary structures, systems, and institutions.

The other levels of morality are also most important for the good of society. The virtues of justice, concern, fairness, a commitment to overcome all forms of discrimination, and a special concern for the poor, the marginalized, and the suffering are most significant for the individual members of society. Social justice from a catholic perspective requires both a change of heart and a change of structures. Neither of these alone is enough. The proper attitudes dispose the individuals to work for more just structures and to work for justice within the existing structures. In day-to-day existence, individuals are called to live out the realities of truth, justice, freedom, love, peace, and a special care for the poor and the needy that are so necessary for the good of society.

Another level of morality concerns the values and general principles that should guide moral life. Members of a society need to develop a common vision of the values that should be incorporated and direct societal life. The values of justice, especially distributive justice and social justice, human rights, and the realization that the goods of creation exist to serve the needs of all, form an important part of the vision of the public good and the good society. The church must inculcate these values as important and strive to make them more present in the perspective and practice of society.

The criterion of catholicity not only points to the many different levels of the moral involvement of the church in human society but also helps point out many of the important problems facing society today and the directions in which we must move. Catholicity, according to our understanding, tries to include all and exclude none. Many of the problems facing society today concern persons or issues that for one reason or another are excluded or marginalized.

The problem of discrimination because of race or ethnic background continues to exist in our world in general and in our country in particular. The erosion of apartheid in South Africa indicates that some progress has been made there. In South Africa the role of the churches has been somewhat ambivalent. Many churches identified with the government and its policies and even supplied theological justification for the apartheid system. Many mainstream churches in the English-speaking tradition opposed apartheid in theory but did little until recently to challenge the government. A few individual white church people over the years have courageously stood up to the government and its policies. The black churches have often exercised prophetic leadership in trying to bring about greater justice. Often in the last few years the catholic reality of the churches has provided leadership in South Africa by giving support and direction to the local church. The recent work of the Lutheran World Federation and of the World Alliance of Reformed Churches has been exemplary.[20] The transition in South Africa will not be easy, however, and the problems of racism and discrimination are not going to disappear.

The inequalities facing blacks in the United States are obvious to all thinking people. In addition, Mexican Americans, Native Americans, and other groups have known and continue to feel the realities of discrimination and prejudice. Our cities are still racially divided in terms of housing and living. In theory the attitude of the churches argues strongly against discrimination and the exclusion of races and other ethnic groups from life in the church and in society. In practice, however, the churches themselves in the United States

---

[20]John W. deGruchy, *The Church Struggle in South Africa,* 2d ed. (Grand Rapids, Mich: William B. Eerdmans, 1986).

have done little to advance the cause of integration. Sunday morning still remains a very segregated time, when people from different races go their separate ways to different churches. Our church practice in general seriously belies our theory of a catholic and universal church embracing all races and peoples. Many factors help to explain the existing situation of segregation within the churches, but the reality stands in stark contrast to the theory of catholicity and universality.

Discrimination in gender has also been rampant in the world in general and in our society in particular. The women's movement and feminist theory have reminded us of the patriarchal structures of our society. Here too the church has too easily been corrupted by the spirit of the times and has accepted the existing patriarchal structures and ambience. Today many churches of a catholic character are trying to deal with patriarchy and discrimination, but problems continue to exist in all churches that are striving to put into practice the recognition that in Christ Jesus there is neither male nor female. The Roman Catholic church hierarchy in particular has alienated many women by its adamant opposition to women as priests and leaders.

Perhaps the most serious division worldwide and nationally is the separation between the rich and the poor. In both spheres the gap between the rich and the poor seems to be growing. On a worldwide scale the economic problems of the Fourth and the Third Worlds are enormous. Liberation theology has reminded us that some causal relationship exists between the wealth of the First World and the poverty of so much of the rest of the world. Trade practices, the arms race, and the international debt of many poor countries have all contributed to the problems of the Third and Fourth Worlds.

In our nation the distribution of wealth continues to point up the growing difference between the rich and the poor. Associated with poverty are the problems of hunger, homelessness, lack of education, drug and alcohol abuse, and inadequate health care. Since poverty intimately involves all those realities that are fundamental to physical existence and survival, the problem of poverty constitutes the most basic problem of inequity in our world.

In theory the Christian gospel has eloquently insisted on God's special care and concern for the poor and the challenge for the followers of Jesus to carry out that concern. The Christian church above all should be the friend and protector of the poor. A Scripture scholar once made the comment that Jesus was accused of associating with the poor, the outcasts, and the oppressed; but the followers of Jesus have striven for over two thousand years to overcome that criticism. Once again the gap between theory and practice is large.

The Christian church in theory has recognized the need to care for the poor. In the course of history one can point to many contributions made by the churches. In reality, however, the church has often sided with the powerful against the poor. To eradicate the problem of poverty today both a change of heart and a change of structures are required. The church can contribute much in both areas. At the present time all of us are more conscious that direct aid to people in need will never address the fundamental problems. In my viewpoint the church alone can never adequately deal with the complex problems associated with our ever-growing poverty, but the churches can make an important contribution in the attempt to change people's hearts and to establish a more just distribution of income and wealth in our country and our world.

Ecological consciousness today reminds us that our all-inclusive catholicity must also embrace the world. We have a responsibility to care for and preserve the environment and to hand on a properly functioning environment to the future. The mainstream Christian churches have generally recognized the human obligation of stewardship for the goods of creation, but too often the environmental and ecological aspects of stewardship have been forgotten. There is some truth in the charge that an overly anthropocentric view of the world too readily subordinated the material aspects of the world to the human.[21]

On the political front today one can see the tension between striving for a greater unity bringing the whole world together and an insistence on national and ethnic differences and independence. Here again catholicism appears to be at stake. The great challenge in our society is to be as all-embracing as possible while respecting the legitimate diversity of those who make up the country or even the world itself. True peace in our world will never be possible until a more inclusive unity exists. However, the threat of a narrow sectarianism and tribalism is omnipresent.

Many commentators today point out that individualism constitutes the greatest danger in the United States.[22] Narrow concern with one's own self and one's own good lies at the heart of the problem of attaining the common good or the public good in our society. True community, with its concern for all, cannot be built on a competitive individualism dedicated to making oneself number one in all things. A truly catholic approach does not deny the rightful role and happiness of the individual, but it sees such fulfillment ultimately coming about in the context of many different associations and communities, including the broad human community.

Christian churches have a name for both the power that tries to dominate others and the willful independence that

---

[21] *Covenant for a New Creation,* ed. Carol S. Robb and Carl J. Casebolt (Maryknoll, N.Y.: Orbis Books, 1991).
[22] Bellah et al., *Habits of the Heart*; Charles H. Reynolds and Ralph V. Norman, eds., *Community in America: The Challenge of Habits of the Heart* (Berkeley: University of California Press, 1988).

wants to isolate and insulate the self from others. We call such attitudes sin. Here again the catholic Christian churches have significant solutions to contribute. The call to conversion and repentance is a call to overcome the sin that severs the bond of love and communion that should unite us to one another and to the ecosystem. Christian eschatology reminds us that the fullness of the reign of God will never be present in this world, but we are all called in theory and in practice to be more catholic by striving to live in peace, justice, and freedom with all our brothers and sisters and with creation.

Different Roles of the Church

HOW PRECISELY SHOULD THE CHURCH BE INVOLVED IN TRYING TO bring about greater freedom, justice, and participation in a sustainable society? One can and should distinguish various roles and functions that the church should play. This section will now develop some of the more significant roles.

Church as teacher and learner. The church teaches and learns its moral understanding of society's ideal structure in a way similar to how it teaches and learns morality for its own community. Here too it distinguishes the various levels of moral discourse and reality. The church must propose specific issues and structures, the disposition of the individual members of society, and the values and principles of the shared vision of a good society. The church here is obviously concerned about its own members, but the church catholic also recognizes the need to be in dialogue with and work with all others to bring about a more free, just, participative, and sustainable society. The teaching function of the church again involves much more than merely proposing certain truths. The Christian community above all aims at the formation of its own members. As history has shown, knowledge and virtue are not necessarily identical. The whole community is involved in this formation process.

One of the important aspects of the formation of the Christian community with regard to its moral involvement in the world concerns the motivation. The motivation of faith provides a strong impetus for one's involvement in working for a more just society. A proper understanding of the tension in Christian eschatology emphasizes the need for involvement in trying to bring about a better human society but also points out that the fullness of the reign of God will never be present in this world. Especially in the contemporary context of despair and cynicism, which has driven many people to retreat to their own private world, the church can motivate its own members with a proper Christian hope. One continues to struggle to bring about a more just society despite all the problems and setbacks. The Christian church knows that it will never be fully successful in making the world more just, but it also knows the imperative to continue to try.

Even with regard to the broader society, one cannot forget that the church is also a learner. History again has indicated how often the church has learned from other people and institutions. The church catholic recognizes that it does not have all the answers but is committed to working with all people of goodwill in an attempt to understand better and put into practice more just human structures.

Church as provider for those in need. Traditionally the churches have contributed to the good of society by striving to alleviate the needs of the poor. Almsgiving has played an important role in their practices. Care for the needy has also taken the form of establishing institutions such as hospitals to provide for those who are sick. The church must always be faithful to the gospel injunction to feed the hungry, clothe the naked, visit the sick and imprisoned, comfort the suffering, and generally bear the burden of those in need. The magnitude and complexity of the social problems facing society today mean that the churches alone cannot adequately deal with them or solve them. The problem of homelessness, for example, requires the involvement of society as a whole and the government in achieving better and more adequate solutions. However, the churches still have some role to play in all these areas.

The churches, like other voluntary societies, can experiment with new approaches and programs to deal with particular needs. If such programs prove successful, then other groups in society and the government itself can adopt them. This was the case with the hospice movement, which began in England with church people but now has been adopted by many others, including governments.

The churches' direct care for those in need still has a great role to play today, but providing helpful services cannot be the only way in which the church structures its mission to society.

Church as empowerer and enabler. Part of the mission of the church to work for a more just society builds on the moral recognition of the individual's dignity, role, and responsibility. The church must work with others in society to empower all individuals to share, participate, and contribute to that society's life. Society does not truly function well if many people are marginalized and do not feel they truly have a voice in their society. The churches can work with all others to empower the poor and the marginalized so that they can more fully participate in determining their own fate and the good of the society to which they belong. Too often in the past a paternalism emphasized only what we could do for others in need and not what they should be empowered to do for themselves.

Church as advocate. In addition, the church should also serve as an advocate for those in need. In a truly prophetic way the church can call attention to the plight and the problems of those who are in need and not recognized by others. The church as advocate can serve to remind not only its own members but all of society of the needs of the weakest and the most invisible of the people who make up the human community—the homeless, for example.

Church as model. A further role for the church involves being a model or an exemplar. First, the church catholic precisely as catholic can be an important model. Both domestically and internationally the divisions within society are becoming ever more apparent. In our country we are well aware of the growing differences and divisions between the rich and poor, racial and ethnic groups, the sexes, and the geographical parts of the country. By our catholicity we challenge ourselves and others to do away with these divisions, which themselves are wrong and unjust, and to accept the legitimate differences so that different peoples and groups can live in harmony with each other. Catholicity by definition calls for an overarching unity while respecting and even promoting a great deal of diversity.

We in the church know how difficult it is to achieve such unity in the midst of diversity. As Christians we are divided along denominational lines. Within our individual churches we experience the tensions and the frustrations of truly being one community. The problems are enormous and obvious to all of us. But if we in the church give up on catholicity, how are we ever going to do better than we do today in civil society? Our fidelity to Jesus and the Spirit, as well as the needs of our modern world, impels us to live out as best we can the catholicity that recognizes overall unity that embraces diversity and pluralism.

Second, in its own internal life the church should bear witness to all that it deems important for the life of the broader human society. Commitments to justice and care and concern for those most in need must above all be practiced in the life of the church itself. From a theological perspective the church itself is to be a sacrament or sign to others of the way in which human beings should live in harmony and community with one another.

The role of the church in working for a better human society, and especially its function as model, recall the sinfulness of the church. The church through its leaders and members might put the institutional survival and growth of the church itself ahead of the faithful witness and mission of the church. One can think here of the many occasions when the church failed to speak out for justice because of its fear for its own institutional survival. One recalls the attitude of many churches to the Holocaust or to unjust political regimes. The sinfulness of the church is also manifested in its tendency to align itself with the wealthy and the powerful so that it fails to speak up for the poor and the powerless. The danger of trying to be respectable in the eyes of the important and significant people in society is ever present for the churches. In its own internal life and in its witness and role in society, the church must recognize its own sinfulness and be aware of its temptations. Many of these temptations are often against the catholicity of the church. Too often the mainstream churches in the United States become identified with the middle and upper middle classes. Catholicity calls for the church to be open to all but in a special way to the poor and the marginalized.

The More Specific Involvement of the Church in the World

THE CATHOLIC UNDERSTANDING OF THE CHURCH AND ITS ROLE or mission to the larger human society recognizes that the church is involved in various ways. Many times the individual Christian will be the actor, either alone in daily life or as a member of diverse groups, associations, and institutions. Sometimes smaller groups of church people will act together. At other times the whole church will be the actor, whether that church is understood as the local church, the national church, the regional church, the universal church, or the ecumenical church.

Without doubt the actor in most cases is the individual Christian, either as an individual or as a member of a group, association, or institution other than the church. The church catholic realizes that it does not take its members out of the world with all its different social, political, economic, and cultural realities. Church members are in the world and participate in all aspects of life in this world.

Members of the church have many other roles, functions, and relationships. Individuals are members of families. The family, despite all its fragilities and problems, remains an important basic unit of society. Family members have different relationships and roles. Individuals and families live together in neighborhoods, which exercise a lesser influence in our modern mobile society but which still play an important role in human social life. People are also involved in the work force in one way or another. Professional groups or labor unions gather people together for self-improvement, for the good of the groups themselves and their cause, and for social reasons. Individuals also belong to the many important institutions that play a significant role in society—schools, the media, and all types of voluntary groups supporting particular causes. People belong to many different social, cultural, political, educational, and recreational groups.

In all these different roles, the individual Christian strives to contribute to a better world and a better society. In speaking about the role of the church's social mission to the world, one cannot forget that the individual Christian most of the time does not function directly and immediately through the church community. Nevertheless the Christian brings the Christian vision and formation to bear on all that she does. In a sense the role of the church community here is more indirect and remote but still significant.

Individuals acting directly and immediately in their own name or in their involvement with other groups and associations are freer than the church as a whole to choose their involvement and positions. As already mentioned, a large area of pluralism exists within the church in which individuals will disagree with others. Total church involvement must respect the legitimate freedom of the believer.

The role of individual church members often working in and through other groups and associations constitutes the primary involvement of the church in the world. The church should strive by every helpful means to form, instruct, motivate, and challenge the individual Christians to carry out their baptismal commitment to witness to their faith in all aspects of their life. At times official church documents tend to so emphasize the role of the institutional church as a whole that they forget the primary social commitment of the church is through its individual members' work in the world in many different ways.

Another form of church involvement concerns groups of ecumenical Christians in general or associations belonging to one individual church working for a particular function or cause in the world. This type of involvement is very minor in comparison with the role of individual Christians, but such involvement has existed historically and continues to have a significant role to play. Thus, for example, married couples, business people, or workers from a particular church come together in groups to encourage one another in their daily tasks in the world. Sometimes people have gathered together around a particular issue, such as peace, the death penalty, or the sanctuary movement. Such groupings enable people who share the same faith commitments to act on them. Since the church catholic includes all aspects of life and recognizes a large area of disagreement and freedom within the church on particular issues, such involvements continue to be significant for a number of Christians. In the final chapter more will be said about the roles and functions of smaller communities within the church catholic even on a local level.

The roles of the total church, whether local, regional, or universal, with regard to the world and the social and cultural orders are varied. One important role, as described previously, concerns the formation and motivation of the individual members. In general the church also contributes to the vision, values, and principles that should be present in the social, political, and cultural orders. In the church's many different functions of influencing, advocating, and empowering, the question arises whether the church as such should become involved in concrete, specific issues. This question has already been touched on in other contexts but will now be discussed more systematically.

Different positions exist within the church catholic on making specific judgments about concrete issues.[23] The church catholic must always recognize the rightful freedom of the believer in these matters. However, as a matter of fact

[23]This question was quite heated in the late 1960s. See, for example, Paul Ramsey, *Who Speaks for the Church?* (Nashville, Tenn.: Abingdon Press, 1967).

churches and their leaders have spoken out even in the name of the church on particular moral issues such as immigration, American military involvements in Vietnam, Grenada, Panama, and the Persian Gulf, abortion, unemployment, and human rights. In general I believe these are legitimate involvements, but they must be done properly. If the position is to represent the church, then it should make sure a truly catholic discourse has preceded the involvement. I continue to insist that unemployment, immigration, and the use of military force, for example, are not merely economic, political, and military decisions. They are truly human, moral, and, for the believer, Christian decisions. However, such decisions involve much data from the particular sciences involved, and any moral judgment that is truly catholic must deal with that data in arriving at its conclusions. Even when all this is done, the church catholic recognizes that because of the complexity and specificity involved, individuals within the church community might disagree with the position. The freedom of the believer in this regard must be protected.

Our experience reminds us of the problems that can arise here. Church bureaucracies can speak out without truly involving the total church. Some people who disagree with the particular approach will tend to feel alienated. The process itself of working on such statements and position papers can be very difficult and contentious.[24] Overinvolvement in a plethora of issues can ultimately reduce the effect of the church's role in society. Yet I still see the necessity of speaking out and taking sides on significant practical issues, provided the safeguards mentioned here are adhered to.

---

[24]Paul Nelson, "Moral Discourse in the Church: A Process Politicized," *Lutheran Forum* 20 (1986): 19–21; Roger L. Shinn, "Christian Faith and Economic Practice," *The Christian Century* 108, 22 (July 24–31, 1991): 720–23.

Other specific involvements by the whole church are more problematic. Should the church as such endorse a particular candidate for political office? Generally speaking such involvements have not been made by mainstream churches that are trying to be catholic. Many reasons support this historical tradition. The church catholic recognizes the areas of legitimate freedom for those who share membership in the same faith community. The church can speak out on specific issues and structures with the safeguards just mentioned. In publicly supporting one particular political candidate, one is involved with many different issues. The complexities are multiplied. In addition, one is also dealing with a person who, like all human beings, experiences the limitations of finitude and sinfulness. Support given to a political candidate embraces much more than support given for a particular issue or cause. From the viewpoint of the church itself, apart from other considerations, the church should ordinarily not support a particular political candidate. It is easier, however, for the church catholic to justify rejecting a particular candidate. The negative is always easier to establish than the positive, as was pointed out earlier. But I think that such involvement by the church, especially in developed democratic societies, would be quite rare.

In addition, the church catholic should avoid any promotion of single-issue politics. The catholic perspective realizes that many different issues face the world of politics and the individual political candidate. To select a candidate or to reject a candidate on the basis of just one issue is imprudent in the light of all the issues involved on the political scene. Such single issue acceptance or rejection of a candidate goes against the catholic perspective, which recognizes a plethora of issues and problems facing society. In addition, political support based on single issues only tends to harm and fragment our political life even more. So many single-issue organizations, groups, and political action committees exist that our political life has become fragmented and shrill. Ultimatums and twenty-second sound bites too often replace political discussion and discourse.

The basic principle of involvement by the total church insists that such involvement recognize the areas of unity and diversity existing within the church catholic. The more specific the matter, the greater the possibility of legitimate pluralism and diversity. In the area of specific involvements in the political order, perhaps the most specific and complex issue concerns the support of a particular political party. Here there exists a plethora of specific issues, many different individuals, and the party itself. For all these reasons the church as such should not become identified with or support a political party in a positive manner. The experience in the United States has generally followed this approach, but the European experience has been different.

Specific church involvement today in working for a better society at times can and should involve an ecumenical basis. The Christian churches share a similar view of what the good society should entail and agree on many broad approaches and strategies. In addition, the problems facing society are so vast that broader support will tend to be more effective. This ecumenical involvement must also respect the different levels of morality and follow the same basic approaches as detailed in this chapter.

CHAPTER 4

Responding to the Challenges of Catholicity

I HAVE MAINTAINED THAT THE MORAL LIFE, PRAXIS, AND THEOLogy of the church should be based on an understanding of the church catholic. In reality most mainstream churches in the United States seem to accept this understanding of the church catholic and work on the basis of it. The first three chapters have tried to justify this concept of catholicity and to spell out its implications for the church's moral life. The main thrust of this chapter will be to recognize some of the challenges to catholicity and how best this catholicity can be lived out.

The significance of catholicity for the moral life of the church is primarily rooted in ecclesiology and theology as already developed. However, the moral problems facing society at large today also underscore the fundamental significance of catholicity. We belong to one human family living on planet Earth with our interrelationships and dependencies. The challenge for our national society and our world is to be inclusive and to guarantee and safeguard the political and social rights of all human beings as we work for the common good of the human family.

The Tensions of Catholicity

But there is another side to the picture. The challenge of catholicity constitutes a daunting task for the church. History reminds us that the church has always fallen short of living out its catholicity. The divisions within Christianity in general testify to this sad reality. Within our individual churches and denominations we have all experienced the painful reality of divisions. At the very least, we must admit that catholicity will never be fully present in the life of the pilgrim church. The moral aspects of catholicity are not as frustrating as other aspects, but the difficulties, problems, and tensions of catholicity in the moral sphere are many. Three aspects—the depth, breadth, and content—of the catholicity of the church in morality will illuminate the perennial tensions.

The depth dimension of moral catholicity refers to the Christian's basic commitment to continual conversion and to live out the fullness of the Christian life. The theological emphasis on continual conversion as part of the baptismal commitment calls for a constant growth in the moral life. Psychological and philosophical studies on moral growth and maturity have intensified the recognition of the need for moral growth and conversion in the life of the Christian and in the life of the church.[1] I believe that all the followers of Jesus are called to perfection and to full moral conversion, although no one ever fully attains the goal of moral perfection in this world. We constantly fall short but are called to strive for a more perfect following of Jesus. This call to continual moral conversion is grounded not primarily in human efforts but in God's gift and call. Some Christians in the church catholic have difficulty with the call to perfection and growth be-

---

[1]Conn, *Christian Conversion.*

cause it appears to give too much to human initiative. However, I believe one can maintain the universal call of all Christians to perfection and moral holiness without falling into Pelagianism or even semi-Pelagianism.

In a true sense the Christian moral life involves an impossible possibility, because as pilgrim Christians we have never fully arrived and will never achieve the fullness to which we are called. The Christian and the church live between the two comings of Jesus and will always experience the eschatological tension of their pilgrim existence. The church catholic embraces saints and sinners who believe in Jesus. Thus the church catholic will always know the catholic and eschatological tensions of being open to all who accept Jesus and the community of discipleship and of challenging them to live ever more deeply their Christian life with the realization that no one can ever claim to have followed all these things from their youth.

The breadth dimension of catholicity with its inclusivity constitutes a perennial tension for the church catholic. No local church can ever be all-inclusive, but each church must embody the thrust to inclusivity in its membership and vision and must especially live out a moral inclusivity in its relationship to the world. The general challenge of catholicity is to embrace all within an overall unity that respects differences and excludes no one. Unity in the midst of cultural, linguistic, and national diversity is very difficult to achieve. No political society in our world has ever achieved such an awareness of catholicity in practice. The United Nations constitutes a very important instrument, but we know only too well its fragility and weaknesses. The church catholic as a whole has not been able to achieve a true catholicity even though it is challenged by its originating vision and impetus to do so.

An inclusivity in the moral life of the church is somewhat easier to attain than an inclusivity on other levels, but the tension and difficulties of bringing about a true moral inclusivity are very evident. A moral inclusivity calls for a special concern for those who are in any way marginalized, discriminated against, or oppressed. The continuing existence of these groups in human history testifies to the difficulty of living out a truly catholic and inclusive morality. The human temptations of pride and selfishness, lack of compassion and concern, and group egoism lie at the foundations of these divisions and exclusions. The divisions of poor and rich; of black, brown, white, red, and yellow races; of female and male and their respective roles in society and in the church illustrate the difficulties in living out a truly inclusive morality even for Christians and the Christian church.

Tensions in catholicity in general and especially in the moral life come not only from the depth and breadth dimensions but also from the content aspects. As described in the last two chapters, the content dimension of catholicity concerns exactly where unity and diversity exist. Proposals were made there to deal with the tensions, but even in the light of these proposals I am the first one to realize that gray areas will continue to exist and cause tensions within the life of the church catholic.

Contemporary Challenges to Catholicity

THE IMPORTANCE OF CATHOLICITY FOR THE CHURCH IN GENERAL and for its moral life cannot be denied, but the problems and tensions of such catholicity have been formidable throughout history. In our own times sharp challenges have arisen to the possibility of a catholicity in general and a moral catholicity for the life of the church.

Many mainstream churches in the United States have been torn by divisions and dissensions precisely over the matter of moral teachings, especially regarding sexual issues (witness the rejection of a proposed new and somewhat radical sexual ethic in the Presbyterian Church).[2] Practically all the mainstream churches are grappling with the particular question of homosexuality, and especially homosexuality among clergypersons. The fact that many Roman Catholics in theory and in practice disagree with aspects of official hierarchical teaching on sexuality is well known. Sometimes these differences have resulted in deep divisions within the churches. One silver lining in this cloud concerns the care and commitment people make to their own particular church or denomination. A few years ago people thought that commitment to a particular church or denomination was dying out. These recent struggles and divisions at least indicate that people take their relationship to a particular church or denomination very seriously.

Significant changes have occurred in the sociological reality of United States churches and denominations that also affect the catholicity of the church on all its levels. Robert Wuthnow in his book *The Restructuring of American Religion* has pointed out the decline of denominationalism in the United States since the 1950s. Denominationalism inevitably embraces some negative aspects but also has the positive function of heightening the commitment to a particular church and the unity that comes from that commitment despite all the differences that exist within the members of the church community. Single issue interest groups cutting

[2]The General Assembly Special Committee on Human Sexuality Presbyterian Church (U.S.A.), *Keeping Body and Soul Together: Sexuality, Spirituality and Social Justice* (Louisville, Ky.: Presbyterian Church [U.S.A.], 1991).

across church and denominational lines have contributed to this decline of commitment to the particular denomination or church. Many of these special interest groups concern matters of morality. On the "liberal" side, peace groups, women's rights groups, and gay and lesbian groups bring together Christians of different denominations, whereas on the "conservative" side, pro-family, pro-life, and pro-American groups exemplify movements which bring together many people from different denominations and churches. For some the commitment to a particular cause or interest can assume more importance than the commitment to the church community as such. The churches both locally and nationally experience the same divisions that face society as a whole and can be fragmented because of these divisions.[3] The proliferation of special interest groups gathered around particular issues and cutting across denominational and church lines makes it much more difficult for the individual churches on all levels to live out the catholicity that calls for unity in the midst of diversity.

These divisions and disputes at least partially contribute to another problem facing the mainstream churches at the present time, namely, declining membership. In the United States the mainstream Protestant churches have been losing members over the last thirty years. Roman Catholic weekly mass attendance declined in the period between 1968 and 1975, but since then mass attendance has remained steady despite great dissatisfaction expressed by some Catholics. The fundamentalist and evangelical churches, on the other hand, have been growing.[4] Thus the expanding and thriving

---

[3]Robert Wuthnow, *The Restructuring of American Religion: Society and Faith Since World War II* (Princeton: Princeton University Press, 1988), especially chapters three to five.

[4]Dean M. Kelley, *Why Conservative Churches are Growing,* Rose ed.

churches in the United States are not the churches that strive for catholicity. Commentators often point out that the more evangelical and fundamentalist churches are growing precisely because they are sure of what they stand for and have a certitude of faith that the mainstream churches do not have. I have maintained that on many specific concrete moral issues the church catholic cannot claim to have a certitude that excludes the possibility of error. I am not defending all the positions taken by mainstream churches on all matters of Christian faith and practice. However, the enticement of certitude that is thought to be behind the growth of the fundamentalist and evangelical churches does contradict my approach to the moral teaching and living of the church catholic when it concerns very specific and complex issues.

The church catholic on the contemporary scene is also experiencing problems stemming from what I can only judge to be a failure to live up to its own catholicity. Marginalized persons such as blacks and women feel that the church has been the occasion and even the cause of their oppression. Such groups consequently feel that they have to separate themselves from the church in order to be true to themselves and to the gospel. Recently this call has come especially from some Christian women who feel very keenly the patriarchy of the institutional church catholic. Some Christian women have formed their own female church communities as their way of responding to the call of the gospel and to the existing patriarchy of the institutional church.[5]

(Macon, Ga: Mercer University Press, 1986); Andrew M. Greeley, *The Catholic Myth: The Behavior and Beliefs of American Catholics.* (New York: Charles Scribner's Sons, 1990), 15–33.

[5]Rosemary Radford Ruether, *Women-Church: Theology and Practice of Feminist Liturgical Communities* (San Francisco: Harper & Row, 1985).

How does one respond to such moves from the viewpoint of the church catholic? First of all, one must recognize the patriarchy existing in the church catholic. The church has been no different from many other social institutions and has been and continues to be patriarchal and oppressive of women and their legitimate needs and demands. The Christian churches today cannot and should not deny their complicity in and support of patriarchy.

By recognizing its complicity in patriarchy, discrimination, and other oppressive exclusions, the church catholic can and should learn something about itself. Catholicity has traditionally been looked upon by some as one of the four marks of the church together with the call to be one, holy, and apostolic. Yet there also exists a fifth mark of the church of Jesus—sinfulness. The pilgrim church is made up of believers who have not and never will be fully recovered from the power of sin and reconciled with the fullness of God's love. The community itself thus is subject to sin.

Christian moralists are familiar with the claim of the early Reinhold Niebuhr that communities and institutions are more prone to sinfulness than individuals.[6] Individuals especially in the Christian perspective have often been reminded of the dangers of their sinfulness and have been alerted to the need to be self-critical. But individuals give their loyalty to institutions such as nations and economic systems that do not have the same system of checks and balances against their own pretensions and sinfulness. All must admit at the very minimum the charge that the church as an institution historically has often been victimized by its own sinfulness and continues to be prone to such sinfulness. The church, if it is to

[6]Reinhold Niebuhr, *Moral Man and Immoral Society* (New York: Charles Scribner's Sons, 1960).

be true to Jesus, must recognize and confess its sinfulness and strive to overcome and change its ways.

The contemporary criticism of the church by some women, blacks, the poor, and other marginalized groups should make the church itself ever more aware and more self-critical. The church catholic is susceptible to infection from sinful attitudes and false ideologies precisely because it is catholic. In many ways the sect is better able to defend itself against invasion by the "world" (in the pejorative Johannine sense of the term) because it sees the church as opposed to the world. The church catholic, as I explained earlier, sees itself in a situation of dialogue with the world. The perennial problem for the church catholic is to be open to the world but also to prevent itself from selling out to the world in any number of ways. Throughout history the church has often succumbed to the temptation of conforming itself to the world in a negative and sinful way. Life would be much simpler if the church saw itself always in opposition with the world, but such an approach is opposed to the very understanding of the church catholic. At the very minimum the church catholic must always be conscious of its perennial temptation of too readily conforming itself to the world (understood in its pejorative sense) as opposed to learning from and incorporating what is good in the world.

Criticisms of the church are often true and on target. Ironically these criticisms from oppressed groups are made precisely in the name of catholicity. The church catholic has not been true to its own purpose and understanding. By oppressing and even ostracizing some people, the church has sinned against its own catholicity. These criticisms call for the church to be truly catholic and underscore the need not to exclude individuals or groups or to pretend to be operating from what is in reality a false universal perspective.

In practice many Christian feminists, for example, have not abandoned the concept of the church catholic. For a time it might indeed be necessary for Christian women to gather by themselves as church to celebrate and live out their Christian and feminist identities. However, such an approach generally constitutes a short-term and partial tactic ultimately designed to change the church catholic so that it will be truly catholic and inclusive of all people. Rosemary Radford Ruether, for example, continues to struggle to renew the church in general and her own Roman Catholic church.[7] One can appreciate the legitimacy of such strategies, which ultimately support and do not work against the proper understanding of the church catholic. Such approaches might be necessary in forcing the church catholic to face up to its own sinfulness and live up to its own ideals.

On the contemporary scene theoretical challenges to catholicity also exist. Perhaps the crux of all these philosophical challenges concerns the very concept of universality which is so closely allied with catholicity. At the very minimum many strands in contemporary philosophy argue against the type of universality that was often used to support moral catholicity in the past. Logically a connection exists between catholicity and universality. A catholicity in moral life and understanding in some ways does call for a type of moral universalism.

At the very minimum many today recognize the historical character of all human knowing, including moral knowledge. The social location of the person is bound to affect one's understanding. We see only a portion of reality and only from our own particular perspective. There is no such

[7] *A Democratic Catholic Church: The Reconstruction of Roman Catholicism,* ed. Rosemary R. Ruether and Eugene C. Bianchi (New York: Crossroad, 1992).

thing as a universal perspective untouched by the tides of time and history. Some of the practical criticisms mentioned earlier arise from the pretense of a false universalism. The white, middle-class male perspective often thought that it was a truly universal perspective but was really excluding many others from its purview. Liberation theologians of all types have pointed out the danger in claiming to have a universal, objective, value-free approach to knowledge. Naive realism believes there are pure, objective facts but epistemic interpretation is always necessary.

Some contemporary ethical theorists have attacked foundationalism,[8] but foundationalism includes a number of different meanings. The common element in foundationalism involves a commitment to certain basic beliefs or principles from which all other justification derives. In theological circles antifoundationalism criticizes both empirical and transcendental approaches.[9] There can be no doubt that foundationalist approaches have often been used to support a more universal and catholic perspective.

Some philosophers contend that identity is tradition constituted. These communitarians oppose the individualism and autonomous reason of the Enlightenment and emphasize the importance of tradition and a living community of tradition. However, no resources above and beyond the different traditions can provide criteria for deciding between traditions or for judging a particular tradition.[10] Similar approaches

[8]For example, Jeffrey Stout, *Ethics after Babel: The Languages of Morals and Their Discontents* (Boston: Beacon Press, 1988).
[9]Francis Schüssler Fiorenza, "Foundations of Theology: A Community's Tradition of Discourse and Practice," *Proceedings of the Catholic Theological Society of America* 41 (1986): 116.
[10]Alasdair MacIntyre, *After Virtue: A Study in Moral Theory* (Notre Dame, Ind.: University of Notre Dame Press, 1981).

exist in Christian theology and ethics.[11] James Gustafson has pointed out the seductiveness of what he calls the sectarian temptation today, which isolates theology and theological ethics from external critical perspectives in order to maintain the uniqueness and historic identity of Christianity. This separation of theology and theological ethics from a broader philosophy or from other ways of understanding our world thus differs from the classic Anabaptist sects but still shares in the separation of the Christian community from the world and from the broader culture.[12]

How does one respond to these contemporary theoretical assaults on catholicity?

The historical character of all our knowing will definitely affect our understanding of catholicity and universality, but such a historicity does not necessarily deny the possibility of catholicity as explained above. First, such historical consciousness makes one more aware of the dangers of a false universalism that also sins against true catholicity by failing to recognize and appreciate legitimate differences. We are now well aware of the dangers of asserting one's own perspective as the universal and all-encompassing perspective. A hermeneutic of suspicion is definitely in order to avoid such dangers. Second, the search for catholicity and inclusiveness must now be much more self-critical and more tentative than in an earlier time, when the significance of historical consciousness was not recognized. Obviously degrees of histor-

---

[11]Stanley Hauerwas, *The Peaceable Kingdom: A Primer in Christian Ethics* (Notre Dame, Ind.: University of Notre Dame Press, 1983); Stanley Hauerwas and William Willimon, *Resident Aliens: Life in the Christian Colony* (Nashville, Tenn.: Abingdon Press, 1989).

[12]James M. Gustafson, "The Sectarian Temptation: Reflections on Theology, the Church, and the University," *Proceedings of the Catholic Theological Society of America* 40 (1985): 83–94.

ical consciousness exist. In fact the three considerations being discussed now are so arranged as to show an ever-increasing degree of radicality. Historical consciousness as such questions a naive catholicity but can be reconciled with a critical catholicity.

Antifoundationalism accepts a greater influence of historical consciousness than the foundationalist perspective. Foundationalism has obviously supplied a strong support for catholicity in the past. Roman Catholic natural law theory well illustrates the connection between catholicity and foundationalism. Roman Catholicism claims that Christians and all human beings share the same basic human morality. The natural law refers to God's plan for the world that the rational creature is able to discover. Human reason reflecting on human nature can arrive at the plan of God and thus know how human beings are to act. The older approach to natural law has been criticized by many contemporary Roman Catholics for various reasons, including its failure to give enough importance to historicity. Human nature was understood to be essentially the same for all human beings in all times and circumstances, and on the basis of this human nature human reason could derive absolute and universal norms for acting.[13] The foundationalism involved in such an understanding is evident.

It is impossible here to enter deeply into the discussion of foundationalism in contemporary theology and ethics. Two points are sufficient for our limited purposes. First, not all who recognize the role of historical consciousness go so far as to reject all foundationalism.[14] Second, those who espouse

---

[13]For the contemporary debate about natural law, see *Readings in Moral Theology No. 7*, ed. Curran and McCormick.

[14]For example, Ronald M. Green, "Jeffrey Stout's 'Ethics after Babel': A Critical Appraisal," in *The Annual of the Society of Christian Ethics 1990*, 27–36.

antifoundationalism do not necessarily reject the possibility of catholicity as proposed here.[15] More needs to be said on this point.

Our social awareness of pluralism, diversity, and historicity has occasioned the contemporary attack on foundationalism. Yet other forces and attitudes are also present. (Note again that I do not necessarily want to canonize contemporary consciousness.) We are more conscious than ever of our interdependence as human beings on planet Earth. The problems of peace, justice, and ecology ultimately involve all human beings on our planet, with their diverse cultures, languages, nationalities, and heritages. The global character of all that we do—life-styles, trade laws, and banking procedures—is readily apparent. The possibility of nuclear disaster raises problems for the entire globe. All human beings must be able to talk to one another and to work out some accommodations so that a free, just, participative, and sustainable global society can exist. The interconnectedness of our persons, possibilities, and projects argues against any tribalism or sectarianism. Human beings in our world have to find some way to talk and work together with one another for the common good and ultimately for their own good. Tribalism and sectarianism are unacceptable options precisely because of the possibilities and dangers of the interdependent world in which we live.

The antifoundationalism proposed in theology by Francis Schüssler Fiorenza well illustrates an approach that does not deny catholicity but actually strongly supports the catholicity proposed here.[16] Reflective equilibrium is a method em-

[15]For example, Stout, *Ethics after Babel.*

[16]Francis Schüssler Fiorenza, *Foundational Theology: Jesus and the Church* (New York: Crossroad, 1984); "Systematic Theology: Task and Methods," in *Systematic Theology: Roman Catholic Perspectives,*

ployed in legal, political, and moral theory as illustrated and promulgated especially in the work of John Rawls. Reflective equilibrium opposes a foundationalism and insists that justification consists in a continual adjustment or correction of our historically conditioned principles and our historically considered judgments. A constant interplay occurs between our commitments and justifications within the context of our beliefs and the search for a coherence among our knowledge, beliefs, and practices. Broad or wide reflective equilibrium recognizes that moral knowledge depends also on certain background assumptions as well as on retroductive warrants. (Retroductive is a philosophical term that refers to an argument that is neither deductive nor inductive.)

This emphasis on discourse and practice for the discovery of truth underscores the importance of community for theological and ethical discourse. Conversation has traditionally been seen as an important aspect in American pragmatic philosophy. Schüssler Fiorenza disagrees strongly with an autonomous, neutral, and individualistic rationality. Rationality involves history, community, traditions, and practices. Constant interpretation through discussion and practice within the church is required for the justification, discovery, and interpretation of truth. Schüssler Fiorenza proposes a catholic community of discourse as the way to arrive at truth. However, Fiorenza also recognizes that such a church community must be in dialogue with all other communities and also with the broader and totally inclusive human community.

Schüssler Fiorenza thus well illustrates that antifounda-

---

ed. Francis Schüssler Fiorenza and John P. Galvin (Minneapolis: Fortress Press, 1991), 1:1–87; "Theology as Responsible Valuation or Reflective Equilibrium: The Legacy of H. Richard Niebuhr," in *The Legacy of H. Richard Niebuhr,* ed. Ronald F. Thiemann (Minneapolis: Fortress Press, 1991), 33–71; also see note 9.

tionalism not only is not opposed to the concept of catholicity proposed here but can strongly support the importance and role of a catholic community of moral discourse for discerning truth. Schüssler Fiorenza concluded his presidential address to the Catholic Theological Society of America by insisting that the community of faith be a community of open and free discourse—truly a catholic community of discourse.[17]

The sectarianism described by Gustafson constitutes a radical form of historicity that sees all reality and meaning as tradition constituted and limited. Such intellectual sectarianism isolates the tradition (in this case the Christian community and tradition) from all other traditions. I agree with Gustafson's strong opposition to such approaches for the Christian church.[18] I do not want to defend all that has been done by the various churches even in the name of catholicity. The last section of this chapter will recognize in greater detail the ever-present danger of subordinating the tradition to contemporary reality and thereby eviscerating the tradition itself. However, the Christian tradition in general and especially in its moral life cannot be effectively isolated from others.

The need for the Christian community to be in dialogue with others and with the broader human community remains crucial both for the life of the church itself and for the broader human community. The church catholic recognizes the need for a truly living tradition. Such a church must be in dialogue with others. In addition, history and experience remind us of the sinfulness of the church and its need to be continually open to criticism from others. The existence of sources and

[17]Schüssler Fiorenza, *Proceedings of the Catholic Theological Society of America* 41 (1986): 134.
[18]Gustafson, *Proceedings of the Catholic Theological Society of America* 40 (1985): 83–94.

realities outside the tradition help to promote such criticism and supply different perspectives for it. The church catholic also believes that God, Jesus, the Spirit, and our faith touch all that exists, and we have a responsibility for the world in which we live. The church catholic has to work with others for the good of all humankind, which never exists in general but in different cultures, societies, nations, and traditions.

Attitudes and Virtues of the Church Catholic

TO ACHIEVE AND LIVE OUT CATHOLICITY IN GENERAL AND CATHOLICITY in moral life and thought will never be easy for the church, especially in the present circumstances. What virtues or attitudes should mark the members of the church and the church itself so that it is truly a catholic community of moral discourse?

Belonging to the church constitutes a basic commitment. For the believer, religion constitutes the deepest, the most encompassing, and the ultimate aspect of life. The religious commitment directs, synthesizes, and gives added meaning to other aspects, commitments, and dimensions of life. In this sense the religious commitment is truly catholic insofar as it pervades all that we do, providing overall unity and direction.

The church is not just a means that an individual uses to have contact with God. The church is more basic than that. Salvation in Jesus and in the Spirit comes in and through the community of the church.[19] Thus the commitment not only to God but also to the church is fundamental. Such a basic commitment to the church is stronger than many other realities that might possibly get in the way of it. We all know and

---

[19]Michael A. Fahey, "Church," in *Systematic Theology,* ed. Schüssler Fiorenza and Galvin, 2:1–73.

experience the shortcomings and sinfulness of the church itself and of other Christians, to say nothing of our own. But recognizing the important role of the church and of our corresponding commitment to it gives us an overriding loyalty and hope that helps us put up with all the frustrations and exasperations encountered in ecclesial life.

Ecclesiology in the United States has often stressed that the church is a voluntary society. This is true in one sense, for one freely joins or becomes a member of the church. In another important sense, however, the church is not a voluntary society in which like-minded people get together to share. The church is understood to be God's way of being present to God's people, and individual likes and dislikes are not the most important aspect of belonging to the church.[20]

All must appreciate, cultivate, and respect the virtues and attitudes that are of fundamental significance for life in the church catholic. These attitudes have aptly been summarized in the classical axiom *In necessariis unitas, in dubiis libertas, in omnibus caritas* (In necessary things, unity; in doubtful things, freedom; in all things, charity). These three attitudes are necessary for the church catholic to function as it should with its overall unity but also with respect for legitimate diversity and pluralism. The problems arise in trying to determine exactly what is necessary and what is doubtful. Chapter 2 has proposed criteria for discerning these distinctions in the area of morality. The basic attitudes do not provide easy answers to the difficult questions of discernment, but they do greatly help the ethos and atmosphere in which such discernment takes place. There can and will be disagreements among church members, but these disagreements must exist within a

[20]Richard P. McBrien, *Do We Need the Church?* (New York: Harper & Row, 1969).

love that accepts and respects the other even while disagreeing on a particular matter. The church catholic can never really flourish without a commitment to these basic attitudes, which make possible the life of the church community. The overarching bond present in all things is charity. Christians have debated from the very first times the exact meaning of Christian love. At the very minimum all can agree that love is not just liking. Loving involves a commitment to and a respect for others. The catholicity of the church community cannot flourish without this unity in essentials, freedom in doubtful matters, and charity in all things.

This book insists that the church is primarily a catholic community of moral discourse, with discourse understood to include practice and actions, so that the church is not just reduced to a debating society. What are the virtues and attitudes that correspond to the needs of such a community?[21] One fundamental attitude involves a true openness to hear and to participate in the discourse. Discourse and dialogue cannot truly occur when minds are closed.

Openness is an important attribute not only of the church's moral discourse but also of the Christian life in general. The fundamental structure of the Christian life is gift and response. Christianity involves God's taking the first step and our responding. The closed person is the one who is self-sufficient, isolated, and cut off from others. From the Christian perspective, such a person is the sinner. Salvation and God's loving gift can come only to the person who is truly open to receive it. This attitude was well exemplified in the life of Mary, the model of believers—"Behold, I am the handmaid of the Lord; let it be to me according to your

---

[21]See also Dennis T. McCann, *New Experiment in Democracy: The Challenge for American Catholicism* (Kansas City, Mo.: Sheed & Ward, 1987), 91–124.

word" (Luke 1:38). From a theological perspective, the call to be open requires a self-critical perspective at all times. One must be truly open to hear the call of God and respond. Proper discernment cannot occur if one is hearing only what one wants to hear.

The other virtues of discourse must also be present in the church community, especially honesty, truthfulness, and respect. True discourse cannot take place without honesty on the part of all concerned. Honest discourse at times will call for the courage to say what one knows others might not want to hear. Truthfulness avoids all deceit, misinformation, and falsehood. Truthfulness begets the light in which true discourse can occur, whereas deceit makes true discourse impossible. Respect for others puts into practice in discourse the overarching call to charity in all things. Thus the virtues and attributes needed for any true community of moral discourse must also be present in the church.

A special set of attitudes or virtues corresponds to the inherent tensions in the very concept of catholicity that have been discussed above in terms of the depth, breadth, and content dimensions of catholicity. To live creatively with these tensions, the church needs combinations of attributes that are often somewhat paradoxical. Let us now consider three such sets of attitudes: prophetic and dialogical, confrontational and accommodating, challenging and forgiving.

The whole church and those fully participating in its life must at times be both prophetic and dialogical. Prophecy has always formed an important aspect of life in the community of the disciples of Jesus.[22] The Hebrew Bible is usually di-

---

[22]See Leonardo Boff, *Church, Charism, and Power: Liberation Theology and the Institutional Church* (New York: Crossroad, 1985); Eugene M. Boring, *The Continuing Voice of Jesus: Christian Prophecy and the Gospel Tradition* (Louisville, Ky.: Westminster/John Knox

vided into three parts or categories—the Law, the Prophets, and the Wisdom Literature. The prophets are literally those who speak for God. The true prophets have constantly pointed out the sins of the people and called for conversion and repentance. In the Christian tradition Jesus was often referred to under the titles of priest, prophet, and king. Through baptism members of the Christian community share in this threefold function and work of Jesus. The history of the church reminds us of the important role played by prophets in the continual renewal and reform of the church. The disciples of Jesus will always be a sinful community in need of conversion and reform. The church constantly needs prophets to prod and challenge and should always pray that the Spirit will raise up prophets in the church to keep it more faithful to its own commitments and witness. The church and its members, in their turn, must be open to hear the prophetic voices and respond to them.

Yet problems and complications often arise. Discerning the true prophet from the false prophet, a frequent exercise in both Jewish and Christian Scriptures, remains a perplexing problem for the church. A hundred years or more of history always makes it much easier to discern who was the true prophet, but the vital life of the church cannot wait that long.

Volumes have been written about the prophetic role and the discernment of prophets. Although no attempt can be made here to develop this topic in great depth, I will mention the primary dangers both for the church itself and for the would-be prophet. First, the danger to the whole church consists in rejecting or neglecting the prophetic voices. The pro-

---

Press, 1991); J. Elliott Corbett, *Becoming a Prophetic Community* (Atlanta: John Knox Press, 1980); David Lowry, *The Prophetic Element in the Church: As Conceived in the Theology of Karl Rahner* (Lanham, Md.: University Press of America, 1990).

phetic message is always disturbing and disrupting. The prophet does not allow the church to continue its business as usual. Because of this, members of the church are tempted to find all kinds of excuses not to heed the voice or actions of the prophet. Can any good come out of Nazareth?

Owing to this perennial reluctance to hear the prophet's call, the church must cultivate the fundamental attitude of openness that I have already stressed. The basic disposition to truly hear and respond to the call of God is vital for the church as a whole and for all its members. We can readily deceive ourselves by holding on to our own narrow visions and accepted ways of doing things. Openness requires that nothing stand in the way of our hearing God's word, including our various attachments and prejudices and any outside forces.

The danger for the prophet is self-deception. Just as the church as a whole must be self-critical, so too the prophet must be self-critical. Those who claim the prophetic role must constantly question their own motivations and actions. The prophet also must be on guard against the danger of self-righteousness. The prophet must always be conscious of personal limitations and sinfulness.

In attempting to discern true prophecy from false prophecy, one must avoid overly simplistic criteria. All can agree that often the prophet is not accepted, but the lack of acceptance alone does not constitute the only criterion for determining true prophecy. Some Roman Catholics claim that the 1968 encyclical letter *Humanae Vitae* of Pope Paul VI, which reaffirmed the condemnation of artificial contraception, was truly a prophetic document.[23] The very fact that so much of

[23]For Pope John Paul II's description of *Humanae Vitae* as prophetic, see Pope John Paul II, *The Role of the Christian Family in the Modern*

the world rejected the teaching is proposed as proof of its prophetic nature. Yet true prophecy could be something urged on the church that would be quite acceptable to those outside the church. Consider, for example, the church's appreciation of the freedom and dignity of the individual in our society. A catholic approach to the criteria for true prophecy must include a number of different perspectives and insists that opposition by the world cannot always be proof of true prophecy.

The church catholic is not only prophetic but by definition also dialogical.[24] The theological basis for the church's dialogical character rests on the fact that the Holy Spirit dwells in the hearts of all the baptized. All those who share in the gift of the Spirit share in the prophetic and teaching function of Jesus. In addition, the church catholic acknowledges that it is in dialogue with, on occasion learns from, and even constitutes itself in relationship with the broader society. The catholic perspective does not understand *world* as a pejorative term, although finitude and sin exist in the world, as in the church. The church catholic, as I have said so often in these pages, must ensure an inclusivity that involves all in the dialogue, both inside and outside the church.

The notion of catholicity brings together diverse and seemingly opposed realities within an overall unity, which the need for the prophetic and the dialogical within the church well illustrates. The prophetic and the dialogical are quite diverse and even opposed. Both aspects must be present within the church. The perennial problem involves knowing when prophecy is called for and when dialogue is in order.

World (Familiaris Consortio) (Boston: St. Paul Editions, 1981), 47, n. 29.

[24]McCann, *New Experiment in Democracy*; Schillebeeckx, *Church,* 187–228.

Such a discernment will never be simple and will always be fraught with tensions. However, an overall unity exists between the two based on the fundamental attitude of openness. A true openness provides general direction and guidance for knowing when to speak and when to listen.

In a somewhat similar way the church and its individual members must both confront and accommodate. At times the Christian is called to confront the church with the truth of its own gospel and even to be somewhat disruptive in the process. At other times the individual Christian accommodates and respects the approach of others within the community even though one continues to disagree. A truly catholic perspective recognizes, tolerates, and even promotes differences when they are appropriate.

The members of the church catholic as well as the total church are both challenging and forgiving. The Christian gospel has precisely this double character about it. The gospel challenges us in our faith and life to be ever more faithful in our witness, but at the same time the gospel forgives us in our continuing sinfulness. We as Christians are called to act toward others in the Christian community in the same way: we are called both to challenge and to forgive. In the very process of challenging we must be conscious of our own sinfulness and our need for forgiveness.

No attempt is being made here to give an exhaustive list of all the virtues and attitudes that should characterize the church catholic and its members. One could readily think of many similar antinomies of the Christian life within the church catholic. The tensions and problems of discerning which of the seeming opposite virtues is required at a particular time and place will never go away. No easy answers are available. In theory and practice, however, some direction and guidelines exist, and Christian love, as the overall unity, embraces the paradoxes of the Christian life.

Antidotes against Inherent Weaknesses

An age-old axiom of the spiritual life calls for one to act against (*agere contra*) a particular defect, temptation, or weakness. Proponents of the ecclesiology of the church catholic must be critical and willing to acknowledge the possible weaknesses and temptations to which the model is most subject.

What is the primary weakness in the model of the church catholic? History and experience point out the ever-present danger that the church catholic will be corrupted by and too conformed to the zeitgeist. The sin of the church catholic most often comes from this reality. The history of the different churches throughout the world and in the United States well illustrates this observation. Too often the churches have lost their gospel values and conformed to the existing cultural and political ethos. Such a problem does not exist for the historical sect model, which by definition sees itself as opposed to the world.

The church catholic recognizes the presence of God in all of creation and so by definition must always be in dialogue with its culture and ethos. At times the church catholic can and should learn from culture and society. Yet in addition to God's creating, preserving, and redeeming actions, our world also experiences its own limitations, sinfulness, and the absence of eschatological fullness.

These three different realities should not be confused. Our world will always know the limitations and finitude of creaturely existence. In itself such limitations are not evil but simply finite. The reign of God can never be totally identified with any finite reality. Human sinfulness, moreover, remains ever present in our world. All can agree with the comment of Reinhold Niebuhr that sin is the only empirically verifiable Christian mystery.[25] The presence of sin in the world (and in the church) cannot be denied. Finally, even those who maintain that God's redeeming love works in our world admit that the fullness of God's reign will never be present in the world. In a true sense nothing human is perfect. However, it can still be good.

As a first antidote to conformity to the zeitgeist the church catholic must be willing to recognize its own sinfulness and its own need for continual conversion and change. Too often the community's recognition of its sinfulness remains a ritualistic recounting of sins and fails to truly vivify the life of the church. The pilgrim church must always be open to acknowledge its own sinfulness and to undergo its own conversion. The church must develop its own uneasy conscience, not in the sense of wallowing in guilt but with the recognition that the church is continually in need of change.

The call to continual conversion means that the church catholic must be self-critical and ready to hear the word and deeds of the prophet. The church community can never become smug, complacent, and self-satisfied. Recognizing sinfulness, being open to conversion and self-criticism, and avoiding the dangers of smug complacency can and should help the church catholic in its attempt to overcome the temptation of conforming to the zeitgeist.

The church catholic should cultivate those attitudes that attempt to expand and promote catholicity and inclusiveness.

---

[25]For Niebuhr's understanding of sin, see Ronald H. Stone, *Reinhold Niebuhr: Prophet to Politicians* (Nashville: Abingdon Press, 1972), 96–101.

The perennial temptation remains to absolutize one's own perspective and to exclude others. The Golden Rule demands that one put one's self in another's shoes, thus preventing the absolutization of one's self and one's own perspective.

The gospel also calls Christians to have a special concern for the poor and the needy. Contemporary theological ethics rightly insists on a preferential option for the poor.[26] In its moral involvement in society, the church must always raise the question, What effect will this structure or legislation have on the poor and the needy? In a society where the poor have no one to press their cause, the preferential option for them serves as an antidote against society's attempt to marginalize them or make them invisible.

Such attitudes are important in the life of the church, but it also needs structures that help the community to be ever more faithful to its call. Within the church catholic each person can experience a particular vocation and call. In addition, smaller groups of people with such similar commitments to a particular vocation can come together within the church to work for their particular witness. These groups thus play an important role in the life of the church and firmly act against any tendencies to water down the gospel call of Jesus.

I do not think that the church catholic, for example, can be totally pacifist. Yet I hope and pray that God continues to raise up individuals and groups in the church who will bear witness to the important value of peace. The church catholic must be open to all the particular virtues or values and cannot absolutize any one of them. Sometimes it might be necessary in the name of justice to use some violence, although the

[26]*Option for the Poor: Challenge to the Rich Countries,* Concilium 187, ed. Leonardo Boff and Virgil Elizondo (Edinburgh: T. & T. Clark, 1986).

church faces the constant danger of endorsing the resort to violence much too quickly and easily. The virtue of peace remains a most significant reality in the Christian life even if the total church catholic cannot absolutize it. Thank God individuals and groups are called to the vocation of bearing witness to this particular virtue.

Voluntary poverty constitutes another such virtue. The whole church is not called to voluntary poverty. Money and wealth are not evil in themselves, but at best they are means that must be used for the good of all God's people. History and experience testify how often wealth and earthly goods have been abused even in the church catholic. The vocation of individuals and groups to live out voluntary poverty reminds the whole church of the danger of this abuse individually and collectively.

These individual and group vocations well illustrate the different roles and functions that can and should exist in the church catholic. I want to avoid the claim that some vocations are higher or better than others. All are called by the one baptismal commitment, but this can be lived out in many different ways. Individuals and groups can be called to bear witness to a particular value or virtue that the church catholic cannot absolutize for all. In a sense these persons bear witness to the future aspect of the reign of God, which can never be perfectly attained in the church and the world today.

In discussing democracy, Jacques Maritain, the French neo-Thomist, recognized the need for "prophetic shock minorities," who exercise a leaven or energy within the democratic society to wake people up from their slumber and to remind them of the ramifications of a truly democratic society. Maritain maintained that by definition such prophetic shock minorities could not be a part of the planned structure of democracy, but the vital life of democracy could not exist without them.[27] (In my judgment Maritain was including in this concept of prophetic shock minorities the community and people's organizations started by Saul Alinsky.)[28]

The church catholic also needs similar prophetic shock minorities. These groups, thanks to the call of God, spring up voluntarily among believers but play an important role in the life of the church catholic. The church catholic must always be open to such groups and facilitate their existence and functions, but these groups come into existence on their own through the call of the Spirit. Such prophetic shock minorities in the church will serve as an antidote to the temptation of the church catholic to conform itself too readily and easily to the zeitgeist and the contemporary ethos.

Ecclesial base communities that have sprung up in Latin America and elsewhere can play a similar role in all parts of the church catholic.[29] Likewise groups such as Women-Church can play an analogous role in the life of the church catholic. These smaller groups are absolutely necessary for the fidelity and life of the church catholic.[30] On the other hand, such groups must avoid the dangers of self-righteousness and must see themselves as part of the broader church catholic. The church catholic needs prophetic shock minorities to make sure that it remains faithful to the gospel and does not become conformed in an inacceptable way to the contemporary ethos.

The church will never perfectly live its catholicity, but the

---

[27]Jacques Maritain, *Man and the State* (Chicago: University of Chicago Press, 1951), 139–46.
[28]See my *Directions in Catholic Social Ethics* (Notre Dame, Ind.: University of Notre Dame Press, 1985), 169–70.
[29]James V. O'Halloran, *Signs of Hope: Developing Small Christian Communities* (Maryknoll, N.Y.: Orbis Books, 1991).
[30]Ruether, *Women-Church.*

goal of the church in its moral life and in its relationship to the broader human society is to be ever more catholic. Such is the vocation we all share as members of churches that claim to be catholic.

INDEX